Preparing and Presenting Expert Testimony in Child Abuse Litigation

A Guide for Expert Witnesses and Attorneys

Paul Stern

Interpersonal Violence:
The Practice Series

SAGE Publications
International Educational and Professional Publisher
Thousand Oaks   London   New Delhi

For information address:

SAGE Publications, Inc.
2455 Teller Road
Thousand Oaks, California 91320
E-mail: order@sagepub.com

SAGE Publications Ltd.
6 Bonhill Street
London EC2A 4PU
United Kingdom

SAGE Publications India Pvt. Ltd.
M-32 Market
Greater Kailash I
New Delhi 110 048 India

Printed in the United States of America

Library of Congress Cataloging-in-Publication Data

Stern, Paul.
    Preparing and presenting expert testimony in child abuse
  litigation: A guide for expert witnesses and attorneys /
author,
    Paul Stern.
        p.   cm. — (Interpersonal violence ; v. 18)
    ISBN 0-7619-0013-6 (pbk.). — ISBN 0-7619-0012-8 (cloth)
    1. Child abuse—Law and legislation—United States. 2. Evidence,
Expert—United States. I. Title. II. Series.
KF9323.S83   1997
345.73′025554—dc21   96-45811

97 98 99 00 01 02 03   10 9 8 7 6 5 4 3 2 1

Acquiring Editor: C. Terry Hendrix
Editorial Assistant: Dale Grenfell
Production Editor: Sherrise M. Purdum
Production Assistant: Denise Santoyo
Typesetter: Christina Hill
Print Buyer: Anna Chin

To the child abuse professionals who do the work
to protect and support children:
May you find the energy,
the perseverance,
and the commitment
to achieve our ultimate goal—
our obsolescence.

And to the children upon whose behalf we work—
for, if the truth be known,
they have more courage than all of us.

Contents

Foreword

It was a jury of average ignorance, perfectly capable of determining which side had the best attorney.

Old Judges' Axiom

Practitioners involved with issues of child abuse quickly discover a reality of their professional life—the inevitability that they will cross the courtroom threshold at some point as an "expert" witness. Regardless of whether that experience is novel, frequently repeated, a voluntary excursion, or one commanded by the necessities of a case or order of a subpoena, the experience often is an intimidating one. Few venues provoke as much discomfort as the witness stand.

Lawyers who employ or challenge such experts seldom appreciate this dynamic. Their experience with experts occurs from the relative sanctuary of their tables in the courtroom, buttressed by their familiarity with the dynamics of court and rules of evidence, confident in the recognition they get to ask the questions rather than answer them. Those days, after all, were left far behind when they graduated from law school and no longer had to endure the Socratic methods of their professors. Only when they confront the need to cross-examine a knowledgeable expert on a subject foreign to them does their comfort level approach that of the witness.

Much has been written in the legal literature about the use of expert witnesses from the perspective of case law decisions outlining boundaries of legally permissible expert testimony. While the law states an expert witness is someone with knowledge beyond that of the average juror, attorneys presenting such testimony recognize the true *expert* as something much more. Knowing the subject may qualify the witness to enter the court, but communicating this knowledge effectively is what defines the true expert. Unfortunately, virtually nothing has been written about how to prepare and present effective expert testimony. This book represents a major step forward in filling this void, offering important practical and theoretical advice to professionals appearing as expert witnesses and attorneys handling these sensitive cases. While the knowledge gleaned from these pages may not alleviate all fears expert witnesses face before and during testimony, it will arm them with resources to confront that experience with skill, poise, and confidence. Attorneys will find this book a valuable how-to manual for preparing, presenting, and confronting expert testimony.

The use of expert witnesses in cases of child abuse and other forms of interpersonal violence has developed out of a social and legal need to attach more concrete and scientific standards to the evaluation of such allegations. Society is uncomfortable with the concept of child abuse, in particular with allegations made against adult caretakers and parents. The problem is compounded by reluctance to make legal and social determinations regarding the credibility of such allegations on a child's word alone. Society as a whole and jurors and judges in particular look for "evidence" considered more reliable on which to base their decisions.

The last decade has witnessed a proliferation in the number of litigated cases involving interpersonal violence, mostly in the areas of child maltreatment and domestic violence. The complexity of issues involved in such litigation, breadth of research, and specializations of professionals dealing with these issues have increased the number of experts called into court. Accordingly, attorneys using and confronting these experts must have a thorough appreciation of how these experts are perceived by judges and juries, and how best to present or discredit their testimony. The fact that the use and misuse of expert witnesses remains one of the most frequent issues for appellate litigation, and a common cause for many poorly reasoned decisions by fact finders, suggests much work remains to be done.

The misuse of expert witnesses has spurred a large body of case law and legal commentary criticizing and restricting the use of expert testimony in child maltreatment cases, especially in cases involving child sexual abuse. Regrettably, such critiques and case law ignore the purpose behind the appropriate use of expert testimony: to assist the fact finder in understanding the evidence or deciding a fact or issue by providing him or her with specialized knowledge. Just as misuse of expert testimony can result in improper verdicts, failure to permit proper use of expert testimony can lead to misinformation decisions based on speculation and bias.

Research on jurors who decide these complex cases reveals that many bring their biases and beliefs into the jury room, and most have little understanding of family dynamics and victim responses to interpersonal violence. Indeed as the author points out, the selection of jurors in the legal system is designed to impanel the group of least knowledgeable individuals to decide the issues. The necessity to educate these fact finders and to do so persuasively become paramount considerations for litigants, most often prosecutors and other government attorneys who bear the burden of proving such victimization to the requisite degree of legal certainty. The art and science of this persuasion are the subjects of this book. Its accessibility to attorney and professional alike is testament to the author's own ability to educate.

Early in their careers attorneys learn that experience rather than formal education is their best teacher. Frequently the most important lessons come from the hardest experiences. Paul Stern shares both his experience as a veteran courtroom practitioner and the wisdom he's gained from successes and failures. Throughout the book, the reader will find practical tips that will improve the presentation of testimony by both witness and attorney and facilitate challenges to improper expert testimony. The author's style complements his message, using clear language, analogies, and repetition where necessary to reinforce points. The book excels in illustrating the substantive message through court transcripts and case examples. Most importantly, the book highlights how to use scientific and social science research and professional literature to support appropriate expert opinions and discredit the charlatan expert.

Chapter Six, authored by Benjamin E. Saunders, provides balance to the manuscript by presenting information and perspective from a respected non-lawyer professional who has had extensive experience as an expert witness and consultant. Saunders accurately comments that the legal profession tends to take itself too seriously, both inside the courtroom and in its relations with non-lawyers, including witnesses. His critique underscores the need for lawyers to obtain the insights of professionals who interface with the legal system. Only through such an exchange of ideas can the legal system hope to balance the frequently conflicting obligations faced by professionals who serve as expert witnesses. Saunders' discussion of the ethical considerations frequently encountered by professionals solicited as expert witnesses is especially important. As is true of most issues involving professional ethics, the answers are seldom black-and-white. For the expert going to court and for the attorney dealing with the expert in and out of court, the time for considering and discussing those issues is well before the first question is posed in the trial.

Readers who follow the author's advice can turn the old judges' axiom around, "It was a jury of understanding, well informed by the expert's testimony, perfectly capable of determining the issues." The "best attorney" should not be one who convinces a jury through his courtroom flair, but one who educates the jury, enabling them to make an informed decision. From this, ideally, the search for the truth will emerge, and justice will prevail.

BRIAN K. HOLMGREN
Senior Attorney
APRI's National Center for Prosecution of Child Abuse

Acknowledgments

Perhaps the best thing about writing a book is that the publisher gives the author the opportunity to include acknowledgments. In theory, this is the place for the author to acknowledge the people who helped in the creation of the project. However, writing this book was the easy part—the hard part was being in the position to be able to do so. That depended completely on those around me who provided encouragement, teaching, and support and led me through doors I could never have opened alone. And so I say thank you to those people here, and especially to three people.

First, I want to thank Irene Weiss and Herbert Stern, my mother and father, for instilling in me the belief that anything is possible and then providing the love and support—and editorial critiques—to prove that it is.

I also want to thank Lucy Berliner, who has been a mentor and friend and who has opened more professional doors for me than I ever had a right to expect. I would never have had the opportunity to do any of what I have done without her help and guidance. I thank Lucy for her belief in me and for her exceptional perspective, which helps me, and I dare say all professionals, to see things more clearly.

Finally, my thanks to those who have provided belief and support in their teachings and in their encouragement, who have provided input for this project and for me, sometimes, perhaps even unknown to them, just by their mere silent presence. Thank you to Jon Conte, Harry Elias, Chris Feldt, Arnie and Sally and Andy Friedman, Brian Holmgren, Kee MacFarlane, Mary Meinig, Jodie Miller, John E. B. Myers, Scott Olson, Ben Saunders, and Murray Talasnik.

1

The Need for
Expert Testimony

What we choose to believe depends on whom we rely upon as our teachers.

Roland Summit, "Misplaced Attention to
Delayed Memory," 1992

Increasingly in U.S. society we require our human conflicts to be resolved in courtrooms. However, those entrusted with making the decisions affecting these conflicts often lack the knowledge base to make informed or sophisticated decisions. They generally must be provided with information that interprets the evidence presented to them and that explains human behavior so that they will be better able to reach appropriate resolutions. Those who are called upon to so educate the decision makers are *expert witnesses*.

The quality of the decisions made by judges and jurors is largely dependent upon the quality of the education they receive from expert witnesses. When expert witnesses are presented by opposing sides, offering divergent information and opinions, judges and jurors must choose whom to rely upon. Expert witnesses must not only educate the fact finders, but must do so persuasively enough to convince the fact finders to believe *them.*

This book is designed to help those who serve as expert witnesses to understand their role and to present their information effectively to juries in cases involving aspects of interpersonal violence.[1] It is also designed to help lawyers use and present expert testimony more effectively, and provides guidance for attorneys on how to identify and expose misleading or irresponsible expert testimony.

The concepts discussed in this book apply generally to both civil and criminal cases and to cases tried before juries or judges alone. Because the rules applying to criminal jury trials are the most restrictive, I draw most of my examples from that arena. As a general rule, if a particular practice is acceptable in a criminal jury trial, it is applicable in a bench trial or civil case.

❏ The Need for Expert Witnesses

In many types of litigation, the testimony of expert witnesses is essential to the achievement of intelligent and just verdicts. Expert witnesses provide knowledge and background to jurors. Without expert witnesses, juries may fail to understand key aspects of the case they must decide.

The court system provides a forum for thoughtful and equitable decisions. At the same time, that system relies upon decision makers who are purposely ignorant of the issues they must decide. The importance of expert witnesses is underscored by an examination of how those decision makers are selected.

THE JURY SELECTION PROCESS

Consider how a jury trial begins. A few dozen randomly selected people are brought into a courtroom. These people are ordinary citizens from a variety of walks of life who have been ordered by the court to interrupt their lives to serve as jurors. Eventually, 12 of these people will be asked to determine whether or not the defendant is responsible for committing certain acts. The process by which these jurors are selected is of paramount significance to the effective use of expert witnesses.

During the jury selection process, these individuals are questioned extensively. The court and, generally, the attorneys ask prospective jurors a series of questions to try to learn about their backgrounds, experiences, beliefs, and biases. The judge has the obligation to excuse from jury service anyone he or she believes cannot be fair and impartial. Additionally, each of the attorneys may remove a specific number of prospective jurors without having to give any reason (these are called *preemptory challenges*). Thus if an attorney believes one of the jurors will react unfavorably to his or her case, the attorney may summarily excuse that juror from serving.

This screening process seeks to eliminate as jurors those with information that may interfere with their assessment of the case as presented in the courtroom. It has the effect, however, of also eliminating as jurors anyone with knowledge of the subject matter at issue in the litigation. If a potential juror has extensive familiarity with the facts of the case being tried, he or she is generally not permitted to serve on the jury. Any individual who knows one of the witnesses, especially the alleged victim or the defendant, generally is dismissed from jury service.

The judge and the attorneys ask potential jurors questions to explore what they know about the subject matter involved in the trial. In a child abuse case, for example, the parties often seek to determine whether any of the potential jurors has been a victim of child sexual abuse. Those who report past victimization are unlikely to be seated on the jury. Those who disclose that they know someone who has been a victim of child sexual abuse may also be excused. Even if a potential juror indicates that such an experience would not prevent him or her from being fair and impartial, an attorney may still remove him or her by peremptory challenge.

If a prospective juror has particular training or knowledge in a specific field of science that might be involved in the case, he or she is generally not permitted to serve on the jury. Thus a psychologist is unlikely to serve as a juror in a sexual abuse case when testimony will be offered regarding the emotional reactions of the alleged victim. Similarly, a scientist is unlikely to be seated on the jury if evidence about forensic testing is to be involved, such as when blood or hair comparisons are used to establish the identity of the perpetrator. The court system thus promotes the impaneling of jurors who know nothing about the potential witnesses, the underlying facts, or the subject matter that will be the topic of the trial.

Although this process is designed to obtain an "objective" jury, it also removes knowledgeable jurors. If, for instance, a potential juror knows a witness, and thus may have some sense of whether that person is trustworthy or not, he or she is prevented from using that knowledge by being excused from jury service.

This process also results in jurors' being prevented from using their own skills and knowledge to resolve the issues involved in the trial. For example, in a sexual assault trial, someone with medical training, who might best understand the terminology used in the testimony of the treating physician who conducted a genital examination on the alleged victim, will likely not be seated on the jury. Likewise, in a criminal prosecution involving an alleged victim who did not disclose sexual abuse for several years, someone who has experienced delayed reporting of sexual abuse him- or herself, or has read the literature in the field about it, will probably be prevented from serving on the jury.

On the other hand, this exclusion also prevents the "knowledgeable" juror from being an independent "expert" for the remaining 11 jurors. In such a situation, the apparently more informed juror may be given greater deference, and thus may have greater influence, during jury deliberations. This can create an obvious imbalance in the jurors' ability to discuss and resolve the case. This is of particular concern because the "juror/expert" will not have been subjected to the confrontations of the adversarial process.

The jury that is eventually selected is one that is ignorant of the people involved, the issues involved, and, most significantly, of the scientific and psychological aspects that might be crucial to an intelligent interpretation of the evidence the jurors are about to hear.

Because the system is intended to have uninformed jurors, it is incumbent upon attorneys to interpret the evidence that is presented to the jury. Any testimony that involves scientific or psychological principles must be explained, and, because the jury is uninformed, the explanations must be offered in a very simple and easily comprehensible manner. This usually involves bringing before the jury witnesses who can help them understand the evidence. If certain psychological phenomena make a person's seemingly illogical behavior logical, the jury must be told why. For instance, a social worker might be brought before the jury to explain the dynamics of why a child may delay disclosing sexual abuse for years, why a repeatedly battered spouse remains in the abusive relationship, or why a long-term incest victim still displays strong feelings of affection for her father.

In other situations, an expert's explanations may be needed because very specialized knowledge is required to understand the evidence. A medical doctor may thus be called upon to interpret X rays, to detail a cause of death, or to explain why certain bruise marks are most likely to have been intentionally inflicted rather than accidentally caused. If a jury hears that the defendant has the same blood enzymes as those found in an evidentiary semen sample, a forensic scientist will be needed to explain the significance of that match.

Expert witnesses, then, present testimony to explain or interpret certain facts or phenomena. They use their technical and specialized skills to explain and reconstruct how events occurred. In essence, expert witnesses are re-creation experts. In a truth-determining process where the fact finders are purposely chosen for their lack of knowledge about the facts, it is vital that they be provided with information that can re-create for them not only what exactly occurred, but, in some circumstances, how and why.

THE LEGAL DEFINITION OF EXPERT TESTIMONY

The rules of evidence allow testimony by expert witnesses under this principle:

> If scientific, technical or other specialized knowledge will assist the trier of fact to understand the evidence or determine a fact in issue a person qualified by knowledge, skill, experience, training, or education, may testify thereto in the form of an opinion or otherwise. (Federal Rules of Evidence 702)[2]

In other words, an expert is someone with specialized experience, training, or knowledge who is able to explain something to jurors that they might not otherwise understand.

An expert is some-one with specialized experience, train-ing, or knowledge who is able to explain something to jurors.

All witnesses are entitled to testify about facts: what they heard, saw, felt, tasted, and so on. In general, however, nonexpert (lay) witnesses generally cannot testify about the significance of those observations. Lay witnesses are also severely limited in expressing their opinions (Federal Rules of Evidence 701). This prohibition includes opinions as to guilt or innocence as well as opinions about the causes of certain events.

An expert witness, however, can offer opinions and interpretations of the evidence. An expert witness is allowed to provide opinions as to the *meaning* of what was seen, heard, felt, and so on. The law deems that, because of the expert's training and experience, he or she will have opinions that are worthy of consideration.

The expert witness can offer opinions based upon facts he or she has personally observed or based upon information provided by others (Federal Rules of Evidence 703). For example, a lay witness may say that he saw purplish bruises on the back of a 2-year-old's upper leg, but only an expert witness can offer testimony concerning the possible age of the injuries based upon their color or explain that, based upon the location of the bruises, they likely were not caused by accident. Such opinions can be given whether the expert personally saw the bruises or merely received information about the bruises from another source.

❏ How a Witness Becomes an *Expert* Witness

An individual can become an expert witness in a trial in a variety of ways. (Exactly what qualifies someone as an "expert" in the legal sense is discussed in Chapter 2.) Most typically, an expert witness will become involved in litigation in one of three ways:

1. by having had direct involvement in the case and relying upon specific information he or she gathered;
2. by having been given select information about the case as collected by others; or
3. by being used to educate the jury generally about a certain technical, behavioral, or scientific issue, without having any specific information about the case on trial.

Most commonly, expert witnesses become involved in trials because of their direct involvement in the cases. For example, the doctor who examined a specific patient or the psychologist who treated a specific client may be asked to come into court and describe what he or she saw or heard or felt, and so on. To that extent the witness is like any other witness. The primary purpose of the individual's testimony is to share observations. However, if the witness has the requisite "knowledge, skill, experience, training, or education," he or she will also be permitted to explain the significance of those observations, and that includes offering opinions. The expert's opinions can often encompass issues that directly reflect on the guilt or innocence of the defendant. Thus a doctor who has treated a physically bruised child may testify about

1. his or her observations of the child's injuries;
2. the biological phenomena that explain how bruises occur and how they age; and
3. his or her opinion, as a doctor, that the particular bruising was inflicted within a particular time frame and in a particular manner, including whether it was caused accidentally or intentionally.

In this situation the expert witness is someone who has some first-hand knowledge of the facts of the case. After testifying about the facts observed, the expert witness may then explain and interpret those facts.

An expert witness might also be asked to testify without any firsthand knowledge of the facts of the case. The witness is instead provided with material secondhand and asked to explain its significance. In this situation, the individual is asked to offer interpretations and opinions based upon the facts as gathered by others. For example, a medical doctor, despite the fact that he or she did not treat a particular patient, may nevertheless be asked to comment on specific findings made in the patient's medical records by others. Thus a doctor may testify as an expert witness to explain the likely cause of injuries based exclusively upon the description of bruising as documented by someone else.

An expert witness may also be permitted to testify at trial without *any* knowledge of the facts of the case. In this scenario, the expert witness is merely offering background material to the jurors to help them understand the evidence. The expert witness might not be asked to offer any interpretation as to the facts of the particular case. Thus in a case where a child abuse victim's credibility has been assailed because she did not disclose all of the facts of her abuse during her first interview with police authorities, a properly qualified expert may be permitted to explain to the jury the nuances of the process of disclosure of abuse. The expert witness is not asked anything about the specific child in *this* particular case. Instead, the witness's discussion serves as general background material for the jury. This permits the jury to put the facts of the case in proper intellectual context.

The rules of evidence permit an expert witness to testify based upon "facts or data . . . made known to him at or before the hearing" (Federal Rules of Evidence 703). This latitude permits the witness to offer testimony based upon materials provided by an attorney, based solely upon a review of the literature, based upon his or her own professional experiences, or in response to hypothetical questions.

EDUCATION, NOT JUSTIFICATION

For expert witnesses to be most effective, they must appreciate the precise role they have in a trial. The responsible expert witness is in court for one reason: to educate.[3] This is true whether the expert is a psychiatrist, psychologist, social worker, medical doctor, nurse, forensic scientist, or any other professional. This is true whether the expert witness is retained by the plaintiff, the defendant, or the court.

The expert witness is asked to provide information to the jury and, when appropriate, to offer opinions about the meaning and significance of that information. The expert witness is not in court to convict anyone. The expert witness is not in court to defend anyone. The expert witness is not in court to justify another person's actions. The expert witness is not in court to excuse, blame, acquit, or condemn. The expert witness is in court simply to educate.

It is the job of the expert witness to explain; it is the job of the attorney to convince. Both expert witness and attorney will create enormous problems for themselves if they get those roles confused. Neither can—nor should—do the job of the other.

The expert witness should approach the task of giving testimony with the mind-set of a teacher. The expert witness must display knowledge of his or her professional field and have the ability to explain it clearly to a jury. The expert witness must believe that the fact finders will reach the proper result if they are properly educated. The expert witness is the builder of an informational prism through which the jurors can see and understand the evidence. If the expert witness teaches clearly, the jurors will hear and see and decide clearly.

The expert witness should give the jury enough information to understand the evidence. He or she must teach the jury sufficiently well that the jurors can use the information to make the proper interpretations and conclusions.

The expert witness should present in court only information that is accepted in his or her professional field. The expert is called upon to inform the jury, so as to help jurors make accurate determinations of truth. Thus he or she should provide only information that is known and accepted. The courtroom is generally not the place to advance or debate professional philosophy. Political viewpoints must be left outside.

The courtroom is a place to teach, and that is the only reason the expert witness is in court.

JUDICIAL EDUCATION

Expert witness testimony may be used in a trial for a variety of different reasons. The primary purpose of expert witness testimony, of course, is to educate jurors, so as to help them understand the facts in the particular case on trial before them. However, expert testimony can play a very important role in another context.

The courtroom is a great place for a judge to learn about issues concerning interpersonal violence. The careful use of expert witnesses is a perfect way to present important information to the judge.

A jury determines the facts in a specific case, whereas judges must constantly make decisions that affect people's lives and safety. This may include determinations of guilt or innocence, the placement of children, the awarding of damages, the appropriateness of treatment, and the severity of punishment. These decisions are significantly affected by what individual judges believe to be true about the subject matters involved. Those beliefs are, in turn, shaped by the amount and quality of the knowledge judges have acquired about these topics.

How judges obtain their knowledge in matters concerning interpersonal violence is troubling. There is very little formal training available to judges on such topics as sexual abuse, child neglect, domestic violence, memory, suggestibility, and mental health syndromes. This means that judges usually need to obtain their education in these areas outside of ordinary judicial conferences.

Most judges want to be as informed as possible in these areas, because this will enable them to make enlightened and appropriate decisions. However, obtaining this education can be difficult for them. (Unfortunately, there are also some judges who are unmotivated to obtain education concerning these topics.) Many of the professional training opportunities available in these areas are sponsored by organizations that may appear to be aligned with pro-prosecution or pro-defense groups. Judges are required to act in ways that "promote [the] . . . impartiality of the judiciary." They have a specific obligation to avoid even "the appearance of impropriety" (Code of Judicial Conduct, Canons 1 and 2), and therefore often do not avail themselves of the many professional training programs in these areas, out of fear that attending might create an appearance that could compromise their reputation for impartiality. Similarly, some judges may consider it inappropriate for them to join specific organizations that provide current literature about these subjects.

When judges do not seek out education on these issues of their own initiative, attorneys may, within ethical bounds, bring that education to the judges. Experts may be asked to testify in specific cases merely as vehicles to provide training and education to the judges.

In a case where an expert witness is called before a jury, the attorney should consider what that expert can simultaneously teach the judge. The attorney may seek to elicit as much background information as possible to educate the judge in addition to convincing the jury. The attorney may introduce specific scholarly articles into evidence, not to go to the jury but simply to be read by the judge.[4]

> *Experts may be asked to testify in specific cases merely as vehicles to provide education to the judges.*

Frequently, the opposing side in a trial will argue that the jury should not hear testimony from a particular expert witness. In that event a hearing (called an *offer of proof*) is usually held in which the judge, without the jury present, first listens to the proposed testimony to decide if the jury should receive it. The expert witness is permitted to answer just about any question the attorney can think of during the offer of proof. Even if the expert witness is not allowed to testify before the jury, the judge will have heard and learned from the expert during the taking of the offer of proof.

The expert witness may be utilized, then, not just in connection with the specific facts of the case being tried, but to provide education for the judge to use in future cases.

❏ **Practical Considerations in Determining Whether to Use Expert Testimony**

The aggressive use of expert witnesses is not without risk. Attorneys should be cautious in deciding when and whether to use such testimony. The use of expert witness testimony may have several negative impacts in a trial. Among the concerns are the following:

- If one party uses expert witness testimony, the opposing side might feel compelled to do the same. This can create a "battle of the experts."
- A "battle of the experts" can create a distraction for the fact finder. Such a battle often results in the fact finder's losing sight of the true issues involved in the litigation. The jury instead becomes focused on deciding which side has the better expert witness.

- When jurors become unduly focused on expert witnesses, they are apt to give too little attention to other significant witnesses, such as the alleged victim or the defendant.
- The use of too much expert testimony can become overwhelming to jurors. They might decide that if the expert witnesses cannot agree, the issues must be too difficult for them, as laypersons, to resolve.
- Using too much expert testimony can become exceptionally boring for the jury. The result can be a jury that stops paying attention or loses interest in the factual merits of the case.
- The use of expert witnesses can be very expensive. Litigation resources may be better spent in other ways.
- There are numerous legal limitations to the scope of expert witness testimony (see the discussion below). The aggressive use of expert witnesses may unnecessarily create appellate issues.
- Expert witnesses might make discovery demands that can result in enhanced trauma and inconvenience to victims.
- An attorney might be tempted to rely too greatly on expert witnesses to "prove" the case. This expectation can lead the attorney to fail to pay close enough attention to other aspects of the litigation. The result, of course, is a case that is not prepared for trial as well as it should be.[5]

For further discussion of considerations in the use of expert witnesses, see Chapter 3.

LEGAL LIMITATIONS ON EXPERT TESTIMONY

Expert testimony may be subject to a variety of legal limitations. Although these will differ from state to state, the following basic questions should serve as guiding principles:

- Will the expert testimony assist the jury?
- Is the expert testimony reliable?
- Does the expert testimony go too far?

Will the Expert Testimony Assist the Jury?

As discussed previously, the standard for the admissibility of expert testimony is whether the expert's technical knowledge "will assist the trier of fact to understand the evidence or determine a fact in issue." Although it is easy to state the rule, it is often difficult to apply it. There is no bright line separating issues that truly need expert testimony to assist the triers of fact in understanding the evidence from those that do not. There are, however, several factors a court should consider in determining whether expert testimony will truly be of "assistance" to the jury in the particular case.

In determining the admissibility of expert witness testimony, the initial issue is whether the proposed expert testimony is *needed* to teach the jurors something they would not otherwise know. If the expert testimony proposed is truly not outside the general knowledge of the layperson, there is no need for expert testimony. But what do juries know about certain aspects or dynamics of interpersonal violence?

Courts and commentators are divided in their conclusions about exactly what jurors know about interpersonal violence. One end of the spectrum has been articulated by the Supreme Court of Pennsylvania. In *Commonwealth v. Dunkle* (1992), the court disallowed expert testimony regarding delayed and incomplete disclosure of sexual abuse by children. "It is understood why sexually abused children do not always come forward immediately after the abuse," the court said, adding that the reasons "are easily understood by lay people and do not require expert analysis" (p. 836). Accordingly, the court held: "We do not believe that there is any clear need for an expert to explain this to a jury. This understanding is well within the common knowledge of jurors" (p. 838).

An opposite view has been argued by a Texas court in a case admitting expert testimony:

> Child abuse, especially of the sexual kind, is not a new problem to society. We have learned, much to our dismay, the problem is larger than ever thought, largely because child sexual abuse was in the past a hidden crime—a taboo topic of conversation. But it can not be said that each of us *understands* all facets of the problem, including why a child who has been abused will act in a certain manner which to the layman may appear unreasonable or inconsistent with a claim of abuse. (*Duckett v. State*, 1990, p. 920)

In the effort to determine what aspects of interpersonal violence are outside the general understanding of the jury, the jury selection process plays a vital role. The attorney seeking to use expert testimony must use this opportunity to establish that *this* jury will be assisted by expert testimony on the dynamics of interpersonal violence. Through the questioning of prospective jurors, the attorney must attempt to ascertain what misinformation and faulty assumptions they hold concerning aspects of the case. The attorney must ask specific questions to get prospective jurors talking about what they believe about particular subjects.[6]

In those jurisdictions that do not permit attorneys to ask questions of prospective jurors directly, an attorney should submit a list of specific questions to the judge, with the request that the court ask those questions. The attorney should also be prepared to explain to the judge why those particular questions are both necessary and appropriate.

The attorney should use the jury selection process as a basis for building an argument to the judge that the information provided by the jurors demonstrates that they are uninformed or misinformed about certain phenomena that an expert witness can address. That misinformation helps establish the need for expert testimony.

Is the Proposed Expert Testimony Reliable?

A second consideration in determining the admissibility of expert testimony is whether the testimony is based upon *reliable* scientific principles. If the offered testimony is of unproven scientific merit, it will not be of assistance to the jury and is thus inadmissible.

Courts will not admit scientific or psychological evidence, even by well-qualified expert witnesses, unless it is found to be sufficiently reliable, as that term is defined in law. The legal measure of reliability is currently being judicially redefined.

The admissibility of evidence based upon new scientific theories has traditionally been governed by a standard called the *Frye* test, so named after a 1923 U.S. Court of Appeals case, *Frye v. United States.* The *Frye* test requires that before a court permits expert testimony deduced from a "scientific principle or discovery, the thing from which the deduction is made must be sufficiently established to have gained general acceptance in the particular field in which it belongs."

A majority of states have adopted rules of admissibility for scientific evidence that are consistent with the *Frye* test.[7] This rule of

Suggested Voir Dire Questions to Help Establish Need for Expert Testimony

- Do you think a child who has been sexually abused will immediately, or at least swiftly, report that to his or her parents? Why? Why not?
- Why do you think it is that in most cases of sexual abuse the child does not disclose the abuse until after a considerable delay?
- If a child has been sexually abused, what external or behavioral signs would you expect to see?
- Why do you think a child might not disclose the full extent of sexual abuse the first time he or she describes what occurred to an adult?
- Would you expect that medical evidence would always be present in a case of sexual assault upon a child?
- Why do you think that medical evidence is seldom present in cases of sexual assault upon children?
- Do you believe that only "bad" people commit these types of crimes; that is, if the defendant has friends, a job, people who like him, that he just couldn't have done these deeds? Why not?
- Have you heard of the term *grooming* in the context of developing a sexual relationship with a child? What does that mean to you?
- What expectations do you have of the type of testimony you will hear in a case such as this?
- Do you think it might be difficult for a mother to, on the one hand, believe that her child is honestly reporting being molested by her father, yet, on the other, not be able to accept the fact that she is married to a child molester?
- Have you read about or known a woman who has been battered by her husband yet remains in that marriage? Why do you think a woman might do that?
- Do you think a child is likely to suffer life-threatening injuries by falling out of bed onto a carpeted floor?
- Did you know that the cause of some injuries can be determined by their location on the body?

NOTE: These questions should be used as appropriate to the individual case.

The rule mandating that no expert can testify unless the theory offered is one of "general acceptance" in the scientific community is designed to keep "junk science" out of courtrooms. It also has a tendency to keep innovation out of court as well. One judge has articulately noted the drawbacks of such a limitation:

There always has to be a first; someone must always be the innovator. Yet, I suppose that Christopher Columbus could never have been qualified as an expert to render an opinion on circumnavigation, and the Wright brothers would never have been able to testify as experts and give opinions relating to flight because, for much of their day, their views never gained "general acceptance within the scientific community." (Judge Stern, concurring, in *Rubanick v. Witco Chemical Corp.*, 1990, p. 15)

"general acceptance," however, has been subject to ongoing debate and criticism in the legal arena.[8] After *Frye* had existed for 70 years, the U.S. Supreme Court, in June 1993, rejected the *Frye* test as the standard for admitting new scientific evidence in federal courts. Interpreting the Federal Rules of Evidence (702), the Court directed that federal trial judges should review proposed scientific evidence and admit it only if it is "scientifically valid."

In *Daubert v. Merrell Dow* (1993), the Court ruled that in federal courts the trial judge's decision to admit expert testimony based upon scientific principles should entail "a preliminary assessment of whether the reasoning or methodology underlying the testimony is scientifically valid and . . . whether that reasoning or methodology properly can be applied to the facts in issue" (p. 2796). The Court set forth several criteria for determining whether a proffered scientific principle is valid, including publication, peer review, potential error rates, the "existence and maintenance of standards controlling the technique's operation," and the degree of acceptance of the theory within the relevant scientific community (p. 2797).

Although *Daubert* technically applies only to the federal courts, several state courts have chosen to adopt the *Daubert* standard for admission of scientific evidence. In so doing, these states have abandoned their earlier reliance on *Frye* or other rules. Some states have revisited their admissibility standards after *Daubert* and specifically elected to adhere to the *Frye* test, whereas others have attempted to intertwine aspects of both. (These rules were being revisited in many states at the time of this writing; readers should be certain to review carefully the latest case law in their own jurisdictions.)

The application of a less demanding standard of admissibility places a greater burden on attorneys and expert witnesses to understand and litigate the benefits and faults of emerging technologies and theories (see, generally, Stern, 1994, p. 5). Attorneys need to learn and be able to debate the merits and weaknesses of the scientific theories presented. Expert witnesses, in turn, have enhanced responsibilities to help educate attorneys and teach fact finders.

Whether a court is using the *Frye* test, the *Daubert* test, some mixture of the two, or a different standard, all states require that before a jury hears testimony about new scientific principles, the theories need be shown to have a certain degree of reliability. This applies to all types of expert testimony based upon novel scientific or psychological principles.

Proving the reliability of the scientific principles frequently requires that a judge hear evidence from the expert witness (and other supporting and opposing experts, as needed) outside the presence of the jury. The judge will then determine whether the proposed evidence is reliable enough for the jury to hear and consider.

Does the Expert Testimony Go Too Far?

Even if evidence regarding scientific principles is deemed to be sufficiently reliable and potentially of assistance to the jury, it may nevertheless still be excluded if it goes too far in invading the juror's role as determiner of the facts of the case.

Expert testimony, although helpful, carries with it specific cautions. There is concern that a jury may be too easily influenced by testimony presented by expert witnesses. This danger has been described by the Michigan Supreme Court in a child sexual abuse case: "To a jury recognizing the awesome dilemma of whom to believe, an expert will often represent the only seemingly objective source, offering it a much sought-after hook on which to hang its hat" (*People v. Beckley*, 1990, p. 404). The Hawaii Supreme Court has echoed those concerns: "Scientific and expert testimony with their 'aura of special reliability and trustworthiness' . . . courts the danger that the triers of fact will 'abdicate [their] role of critical assessment' and 'surren-der . . . their own common sense in weighing testimony' " (*State v. Batangan*, 1990, p. 51).

Expert testimony, therefore, needs to be limited to providing the jury with information; experts cannot provide specific answers. Ex-pert witnesses are usually unable to testify, for example, that a specific individual *was* sexually assaulted, or that a particular indi-vidual is the likely perpetrator. It is generally inappropriate for a witness to rely upon scientific theories to testify that a particular witness is telling the truth.[9] Expert witness testimony is usually restricted to prevent the expert from making any comment about the credibility of a witness or a party.

When expert witnesses have gone too far in this area, appellate courts have been quick to criticize. The frustration of appellate courts in seeking to limit expert witnesses from testifying as to whether they believed a particular witness was being truthful was perhaps never clearer than in *State v. Milbradt* (1988). There the Oregon Supreme Court reversed a conviction in a sexual abuse case and made very plain its directive to trial judges:

> We have said it before, and we will say it again, but this time with emphasis—we really mean it—*no psychotherapist may render an opinion on whether a witness is credible in any trial conducted in this state.* The assessment of credibility is for the trier of fact and not for psychothera-pists. (p. 624)

Expert witnesses are similarly restricted, generally, from offering any opinion as to the guilt or innocence of a particular party. This was the specific concern of the Kansas Supreme Court, for example, in reversing convictions in a child sexual abuse case. The court ob-served: "Here the [expert] witnesses attempted to serve as human lie detectors for the child and both told the jury that in their professional opinions the child was truthful and the defendant was guilty as charged" (*State v. Jackson*, 1986, p. 238).

Expert witnesses are also strictly prohibited from testifying that the defendant fits (or fails to fit) an "offender profile." This is based in part on the fact that there is no scientific validity that any such profile exists (see Murphy & Peters, 1992).[10] Courts are also concerned that such evidence does nothing more than try to establish guilt by the defendant's status within a group of statistically likely molesters (see, e.g., *State v. Maule*, 1983).

The scope of what expert witnesses are permitted to say differs from state to state. The expert witness must be carefully counseled by the presenting attorney as to the legal limitations of the scope of his or her testimony. The attorney must be aware of these legal limitations and must clearly communicate them to the expert witness. The expert witness, in turn, must be careful not to testify in a way that exceeds what is scientifically provable. This will be easier when both attorney and witness remember that the only task of the expert witness is *to educate*.

❏ **Notes**

1. Usually, it is a jury that decides the facts in a trial. In some instances, the judge, and not a jury, serves as the fact finder. Unless otherwise specified, I will use the words *jury* and *juror* throughout this volume to denote the fact finder in a trial, be it judge or jury.

2. The Federal Rules of Evidence apply only to federal courts, but the majority of states have adopted evidence codes that very closely follow the federal rules.

3. This discussion is premised on the notion that those who testify as expert witnesses will do so ethically and responsibly. Of course, the reality is that there are those who choose to perform the role of expert witness without adherence to these principles. There are those who place personal monetary considerations or their own political or philosophical agendas ahead of their ethical responsibilities. Those individuals are more accurately "advocates in experts' clothing." The identification and exposure of these individuals is vital for the good of all professionals. Chapter 7 shares at length some thoughts on accomplishing this.

4. In fact, such articles (termed "learned treatises" in the Federal Rules of Evidence 803[18]) should *not* go to the jury.

5. For some thoughtful discussion of the appropriate use of expert witness testimony, see Myers et al. (1989).

6. Such questioning is proper so long as it does not rise to the level of an emotional appeal (*Townsend v. State*, 1987).

7. As of the end of 1993, 16 of the 36 states that had enacted rules of evidence analogous to the Federal Rules of Evidence continued to follow *Frye*; 12 states have applied the *Frye* test without having adopted the Federal Rules of Evidence.

8. For a judicial review of these arguments, see *People v. Leahy* (1994).

9. Following *Daubert v. Merrell Dow*, renewed efforts have been made to introduce polygraph test results. See, for example, *U.S. v. Crumby* (1995).

10. One case has permitted such profile evidence: *People v. Stoll* (1989). However, this case not only represents a significantly minority view, it is also inconsistent with other cases from the state. For discussion of this issue, see U.S. v. Pierre (1987).

2

Who Are the Experts?

The law extends equal dignity to the opinions of charlatans and Nobel Prize winners.

> Donald Elliott, "Science Panels in Toxic
> Tort Litigation," 1987

An expert witness is someone with specialized knowledge, skill, experience, training, or education who is able to explain to jurors something important about the litigation that they might not otherwise understand. The expert witness must be an educator, interpreter, and explainer. The effective expert witness must also be smart, informed, thorough, articulate, savvy, and attentive. Who is capable of filling this role?

❏ **An Expert Need Not Be *the* Expert**

There is a significant difference between being an expert in the professional field in which one practices and being an expert in court. In the witness's field of practice, the "experts" are generally thought of as those who have written the textbooks or who are particularly well known and held in high esteem by their peers. The "expert" is considered to be someone who has lectured for years or who is acclaimed for a significant discovery or advancement in the field.

In the courtroom, the standard for being termed an expert is substantially less demanding. To qualify as an expert witness, the individual need not be *the* expert in the field; he or she need only have sufficient specialized knowledge and/or experience to provide testimony that will be "helpful" to the jury.

As I noted in Chapter 1, during the jury selection process, individuals with knowledge about the technical subjects involved in a case are likely to be excused from jury service. Because the purpose of expert testimony is to provide education to an uninformed jury, the amount of expertise an individual needs to be considered an expert in court is not much more than would have disqualified him or her from serving as a juror in the case.

Whether a witness qualifies as an expert is a matter left to the discretion of the trial judge. Judges generally follow the principle that "it is for the jury to determine the credibility, weight and probative value of the expert's testimony" (*Rubanick v. Witco Chemical Corp.*, 1990, p. 4).[1] Many courts resist acting as strict gatekeepers of expert testimony, preferring to admit expert testimony with the belief that the jury will "give it the weight it deserves."

It appears that the judicial trend is toward a lowering of the threshold for the admissibility of scientific evidence. The U.S. Supreme Court ruling in *Daubert v. Merrell Dow* (1993) will make it easier for junk science to be admitted in court (see the discussion in Chapter 1); with increased junk science also comes a likely increase in junk scientists.

The extent of the qualifications possessed by a particular expert witness, therefore, affects the value the jury will place on the witness's testimony. Jurors are free to put whatever weight and reliance on expert witnesses' testimony they deem appropriate. Jurors are generally given directions by the judge as to how to evaluate the testimony of experts. These instructions differ from jurisdiction to jurisdiction, but many are similar in substance to this one, which is used in federal courts:

> You have heard testimony from persons described as experts. Persons who, by education and experience, have become expert in some field may state their opinion on matters in that field and may also state their reasons for the opinion.
>
> Expert opinion testimony should be judged just like any other testimony. You may accept it or reject it, and give it as much weight as you think it deserves, considering the witness's education and experience, the reasons given for the opinion, and all the other evidence in the case. (*Model Criminal Jury Instructions*, 1994, Criminal Instruction 4.16 Opinion Evidence, Expert Witness)

Given these factors as a guide, the attorney must give the jury reasons to want to rely upon the opinions and teachings of the expert witness he or she is presenting.

❏ Establishing the Qualifications of an Expert Witness in Court

In presenting expert testimony, a determination has been made that the jury needs guidance to resolve an issue at stake in the litigation. Frequently the issue involved is at the core of the case. The expert witness is called to testify to help the jury understand or interpret certain evidence. For the testimony to be of value, the jury must have confidence in the knowledge, opinions, and credibility of the expert witness. One of the most important factors in gaining the jury's confidence is the manner in which the qualifications of the expert witness are set forth in court. Special attention must be paid to how the expertise of the witness is established for the jury.

The expert is first introduced to the jury through the presentation of his or her credentials. During this introductory phase, the jurors measure the witness's demeanor, professionalism, and ego. It is at

"May I ask you to call for quiet, Your Honor? My
witness is about to share his expertise."

this point that they determine whether or not this is someone whose opinions they want to rely upon.

This first impression is especially critical when there will be conflicting expert witnesses offered by the opposing parties. The experts are likely to offer different viewpoints and to present contradictory interpretations of the facts. Jurors are apt to decide the case based upon who they believe is the "better" expert. (Methods to enhance the effectiveness of the *content* of the testimony of the expert witness are discussed in detail in Chapter 4.)

Jurors may also have enhanced expectations of the qualifications of expert witnesses based upon media coverage of recent high-profile trials. The expert witness, therefore, must not only educate jurors, but convince them that he or she should be trusted and believed. In presenting expert testimony, the attorney must present the expert witness in a way that motivates the jury to accept completely what the witness says.

> *The expert witness must not only educate jurors, but convince them that he or she should be trusted.*

An expert witness may have spectacular qualifications—the attorney may know that and the expert's professional peers may know that. But those qualifications are impressive only to those with sufficient knowledge to appreciate them. Such credentials as serving as editor of a professional journal, founding an organization, and winning particular awards are important only if the *jury* understands they are important. It is therefore incumbent upon the attorney not just to provide the expert witness's qualifications, but to do so in such a way that the jury understands *why* they are important.

All too often, the attorney merely asks the expert witness to list his or her professional accomplishments and involvements and then moves on to "the important stuff." This mechanical recitation of credentials is of minimal value for establishing the true reliability of the witness in the mind of the jury.

Following are two examples of the presentation of testimony to a jury about the qualifications of a particular expert witness (the examples address just two areas: the witness's professional associations and publications). Assume that the witness belongs to some appropriate professional organizations, has published five professional articles, and has been asked to serve as a peer reviewer for others. The first exchange illustrates an ineffective method of presenting the expert's qualifications (note the witness's anticipated brief answers):

Question: Doctor, do you belong to any professional organizations?
Answer: Yes I do.
Question: Would you please tell the jury what professional organizations you are a member of?
Answer: [Lists organizations.]
Question: And doctor, have you published any articles in this field?
Answer: Yes I have.
Question: How many?
Answer: Five.
Question: Would you please list for the jury the names of the articles you have published?
Answer: [Reads titles.]

The attorney now thinks that he or she is done.

The second exchange illustrates a more effective method:

Question: Doctor, in your field, are there certain professional organizations practitioners can elect to join?
Answer: Yes, there are.
Question: Why would someone elect to belong to a professional organization?
Answer: It is a way of staying current in the field. These organizations often provide professional journals and hold annual conferences.
Question: What would you consider the leading professional organizations in your area of practice?
Answer: [Lists them, including organizations X, Y, and Z.]
Question: Are you required to belong to these organizations?
Answer: No. It is something I do to further my knowledge of the advances in the field in which I practice.
Question: Have you chosen to belong to any of those professional organizations?
Answer: Yes I have. I belong to X, Y, and Z. I also belong to [lists them].
Question: Doctor, you mentioned that professional organizations often provide journals. What is a professional journal?

Answer: Journals are like magazines for the professional. They contain scholarly articles on subjects of concern to the field. These articles are generally written by the world's leading researchers and practitioners within the particular discipline.

Question: Why would someone read those articles?

Answer: To improve their skills, knowledge, and practice. These journals allow practitioners to stay abreast of the most recent research and thinking in the field.

Question: Well, who writes those articles?

Answer: Usually they are submitted by the top people in the field. Sometimes the journal editors will seek out a particularly well regarded expert to write about a topic.

Question: You said people can submit articles. Are they then published like a letter to the editor? That is, if someone has an idea and sends it in, it gets published in these journals?

Answer: No. Almost all professional journals, and certainly the well-respected ones, require that all submitted articles go through what is called a peer review process.

Question: What is peer review?

Answer: [Describes process.]

Question: Who are these peer reviewers?

Answer: They are people usually well known in the field who the journal editor believes are among the brightest and most informed professionals in the field.

Question: Why do articles go through peer review?

Answer: To make sure that before anything is published it is deemed accurate, reliable, and of value to other professionals in the field.

Question: So by reading professional journals are you able stay current in the state of knowledge in the field in which you practice?

Answer: I believe so.

Question: And by reading these professional journals are you able to stay current in the latest research and advanced thinking of the top people in field?

Answer: That is my intention.

Question: How many professional journals do you get?

Answer: [Gives number.]

Question: How often do you read them?

Answer: [Gives reasonable time frame.]

Question: Why?

Answer: So I can attempt to stay as current in the literature and the advancements in the field as I can. I take this responsibility very seriously.

Question: You said another reason that you belong to professional organizations was to attend conferences?

Answer: That's right.

Question: What are professional conferences?

Answer: [Explains.]

Question: Why go?

Answer: Usually at these conferences the leading people in the field come to present their work [etc.].

Question: How are the speakers for these conferences selected?

Answer: The conference organizers usually seek the most respected people in the field to present at the conferences.

Question: Have you ever presented at any conferences?

Answer: Yes. I have presented at approximately [x number] of conferences. . . . [Lists subjects if germane to subject of testimony.]

Question: So, have your peers recognized you as someone who is so respected in this field that you were invited to present at national conferences?

Answer: Well, yes.

Question: Where did you present?

Answer: [Lists states.]

Question: You mentioned earlier that professional journals publish articles from the leading practitioners and researchers in the field. Have you ever published any articles?

Answer: Yes I have.

Question: In what journals?

Answer: [Lists them.]

Question: Are those considered prestigious journals in your field?

Answer: Yes.

Question: So people who subscribe to these journals in a desire to improve their knowledge and skills would be learning from you?

Answer: They would.

Question: Would you please summarize for the jury what these articles are about?

Answer: [Lists articles and provides very brief summaries, focusing on the relevance to the subject matter of the testimony.]

Question: Were these articles subject to peer review?

Answer: Yes.

Question: You mentioned earlier that peer reviewers are those who are regarded as the top experts in the field. For each article you wrote, did the peer reviewers examine your work and find it accurate and worthy of being shared with other professionals in the field?

Answer: Yes. All the articles I have published have been subject to peer review. Also, I have not submitted any article for publication and had it rejected by the peer reviewers or editors.

Question: Have you ever been asked to peer review articles written by others?

Answer: Yes.

Question: For what journals?

Answer: [Lists them.]

Question: You mentioned earlier that the journal editors select as peer reviewers those they consider the top authorities in the country in the particular field.

Answer: Yes.

Question: And you have been asked to serve as a peer reviewer how many times?

Answer: [X number] times.

Which presentation is likely to be more persuasive to the jury? Which is likely to lead the jury to have enhanced confidence in the witness's opinion?

The above examples illustrate how the witness's experience of publishing and reviewing articles may be presented in a way that demonstrates that such activity means something: that the expert is deemed by his or her peers to be respected, informed, and worthy of learning from.

To accomplish this, the presentation of the expert witness's credentials may sometimes be extensive. In one case, for instance, a clinical psychologist was called as an expert witness to testify about issues in treating sex offenders. The witness had extraordinary credentials and the attorney apparently shared all of them. The court noted: "Her testimony regarding her qualifications covers fifty-three pages of transcript, and it consumed about one and one-half hours of court time" (*Duchess County Dept. of Social Services v. Mr. G.*, 1988, n. 1).[2] In ruling on behalf of the side that presented this witness, the court concluded that it was relying upon that expert's opinions, as they were "anchored by the strength and breadth of her experience and her credentials."

In other circumstances, however, it is unwise to present each and every one of an expert witness's credentials. In a case tried by a jury, this might have the result of putting them to sleep; in a case tried by a judge, he or she is going to have the witness's curriculum vitae in hand. It is recommended that the attorney highlight only those aspects of the expert witness's qualifications that are relevant to the issue being litigated. For example, in a case of sexual abuse of a 12-year-old boy, a key issue in the jury trial was the medical significance of injuries seen around the child's anus. The expert was asked to discuss her qualifications in regard to her expertise to conduct and interpret anal exams. This included the following exchange:

Question: Is there a specialized training that is available in this state for pediatricians to go through if they want additional expertise in child sexual abuse examinations?
Answer: Yes, there is.
Question: . . . Have you gone through that training?
Answer: I have. [Witness then described the program.]
. . .
Question: And do those people with expertise in particular areas come in to address particular areas?
Answer: Yes.
Question: Is there a particular part of that training that deals exclusively with anal findings?
Answer: Yes.
Question: That is damage to the anus?
Answer: Yes.
Question: And did you attend that particular training?
Answer: I did.
. . .
Question: . . . Have you ever done any training yourself?
Answer: Yes.
Question: With other doctors?
Answer: Yes. [Witness then described a specific training program that had recently been held.]
Question: Did other doctors participate?
Answer: Yes.

Question: And, again, did they get [it] set up so that certain doctors presented [within their] particular areas of expertise?
Answer: Yes.
Question: What area did you present in?
Answer: I presented anal findings . . . .[3]

In presenting the expert's credentials, the attorney must establish the witness as someone deserving of the jury's belief and trust in the area to be discussed in the case. Merely asking the witness to "tell the jury about your credentials" is not sufficient.

THE EXPERT'S CURRICULUM VITAE

Before the attorney can discuss all of the significant credentials of the expert witness, he or she, of course, must be informed of them in advance of trial. It is an obligation of the witness, therefore, to provide that information to counsel before trial.

Every professional should maintain a curriculum vitae for use exclusively in court. The purpose of this CV is to document all of the professional associations and accomplishments of the witness; a copy of it should be provided to the attorney before trial.

A court curriculum vitae is very different from a job-seeking résumé. A job-seeking résumé is intended to promote the candidate by highlighting his or her professional career. It may contain language discussing the professional and future goals of the job candidate. This type of résumé should not be used in a courtroom.

An alternative to maintaining a court CV is to keep a court file, either on paper or on computer. All of the information detailing the witness's training, experience, affiliations, publications, and so on goes into such a file. The assembled information can then be shared with the attorney pretrial, without the drafting of a specific document.

A professional should include in his or her curriculum vitae or court file *every* professional conference attended, every article written, every workshop given. Whenever he or she joins a professional organization, is appointed to a committee, or engages in any similar professional activity, that information should be included in the CV or added to the court file.

The witness should remember that the purpose of a court curriculum vitae is to inform the jury of his or her professional involvements. Jurors are very unlikely to have engaged in any professional activity in the expert's field of practice. Thus, even if the professional does not believe that an article he or she has published or a conference he or she has attended was particularly outstanding, if it is relevant to the professional's field of practice, it should be added to the court CV. Although it may not be a great professional accomplishment, it remains one achievement more than the jurors have obtained.

In preparing for court, the witness and the attorney will decide which specific items on the curriculum vitae will be highlighted in the context of the particular case. (In front of the jury, the attorney should go through the credentials of the expert witness verbally, and *not* just mark and introduce the CV as an exhibit. Once the document is marked, an attorney may be prevented from further discussing the qualifications of the witness by a judge who deems the testimony to be cumulative.)

The curriculum vitae should be thorough and complete. It is also imperative that it be accurate. A witness should *never* add something to his or her curriculum vitae that is not 100% correct. Prior to each court appearance, the witness *must* carefully review the document to make certain that it is not only complete but current. As will be discussed more fully in Chapter 7, there is no quicker way to be discredited as an expert witness than to include things on a CV that are inaccurate.

This point can be illustrated by the simplest of examples. If the witness once belonged to an organization but that membership has lapsed, then that membership should not be listed on the court curriculum vitae. In preparing a cross-examination, one of the easiest items for an opposing attorney to check is the status of membership in professional organizations. If the witness claims to be a member of an organization and at the time of trial is not, the witness's credibility can be immediately diminished. This concern is equally true for all other aspects of the professional's credentials. What is listed must be completely precise and accurate. When the CV is not accurate, the results can be humiliating.

Question: Doctor, we were talking before the noon recess about some errors in your CV, the fact that you're not a certified sex therapist by this organization anymore and that's inaccurate and we talked about the fact that your employment in Everett is left off of here. I want to pick up on that theme, inaccuracies. . . . Have you had a chance to look through your résumé again, your CV recently? I'll give it to you.

Answer: Yeah.

Question: So maybe you can just save us all some time and tell us if there are other things in there that in fact really aren't accurate anymore. [Handing CV to witness.]

. . .

Question: So which one should we eliminate?

Answer: Association for the Advancement of Psychology. I don't think it's current. Academy of Behavior Medicine, geez, they just. . . . You know, that was mainly for certification. So I don't belong to the agency, but they did certify me as a diplomate. In fact, I think they just recently sent me an updated diploma. But I'm not, you know, I don't continue to function in the organization.

American College of Forensic Psychology. I'm not sure I went to the last conference, so I don't know if I paid dues for this year. But ABM is definitely not one that I'm doing now. . . .

Question: Okay, so there are, in the list here of professional memberships and certifications there are some things that are outdated and no longer current.

Answer: Yes. It should be updated.

Question: So reliance on these would really be inaccurate.

Answer: Probably.

SOURCE: Testimony of proposed defense expert witness in *State v. Werlein* (November 3, 1989).

In the earlier illustration of a direct examination establishing the professional qualifications of the expert witness, the attorney focused on a few specific areas of professional credentials. Among other professional credentials that might be explored are the following:

- Education
- Dissertation papers
- Internships (not only where but in what and with whom, if relevant)
- Specialized training, including professional conferences attended
- Fellowships
- Academic awards
- Affiliations with professional organizations
- Board memberships
- Grants ("Do you mean that government agencies reviewed your proposed work, compared it with other research proposals, and elected to give *you* money to conduct further research in this field?")
- Board certifications (especially nonmandated certifications)
- Licensures
- Professional committees/commissions on which the witness serves (Is membership a result of volunteering, appointment, or election?)
- Jobs held, experience in the field
- Work as a consultant
- Advisory boards ("They sought *you* out for advice?")
- Papers published
- Research conducted
- Book chapters written
- Peer review of professional articles
- Editorial positions on journals or for books
- Workshops and other training provided
- Keynote addresses or other speeches given
- Professional awards received
- Faculty positions held
- Prior qualification in court as an expert witness
- Legislative testimony given

Not all of these need be discussed by the witness. However, the attorney might look to these, and similar items, to determine what qualifications the particular witness possesses that will best enhance the witness's credibility. In each case the attorney should emphasize only those credentials that are most germane to the issues involved in the trial. Those that are addressed in court should be the ones that tend to give the jury greater reason to accept the teaching and opinions of the witness in the specific case.

❑ Even Without Credentials, Experience Alone Does It

A person's qualifications to be an expert may include education and training. However, to qualify as an expert a witness does not need to have been published and need not have taught, received a graduate degree, or accomplished any great deed. Experience alone can be sufficient to establish expertise.

The rule in every state is consistent with this statement by the Washington Supreme Court: "Practical experience in a given area can qualify a witness as an expert" (*State v. Smith*, 1977). For example, in a child molestation case, a Department of Family and Children's Services worker was qualified to testify as an expert on certain behaviors of a child, even though the witness had no training as a psychologist. Her experience and the fact that she had attended seminars were sufficient (*Kelly v. State*, 1990). Likewise, a police detective was considered sufficiently qualified as an expert on the child sexual abuse accommodation syndrome by virtue of his training courses and work experience (*State v. St. Hilaire*, 1989).

❑ Don't Get Carried Away

A special caution must be made here. As I have noted, qualification as an expert witness in court does not require a high degree of professional credentials. However, an expert must be careful not to offer testimony in areas in which he or she is not an expert.

A witness who is qualified as an expert in one area might find it enjoyable to be asked his or her opinion. Such a witness could be tempted to offer opinions about other topics, and might start to testify as an expert in a related but slightly different field.

The expert witness must be careful not to exceed the limits of his or her field of professional practice. Just because the witness is deemed an expert in one area, this does not

The expert witness must be careful not to exceed the limits of his or her field of professional practice.

An example of a witness who strayed from his field of expertise is provided here in an excerpt from an actual court transcript. The witness, a child psychiatrist by training, was seeking to testify in a child abuse case interpreting *medical* evidence, including colposcopic slides. Although the doctor had some prior medical training, this was obviously not his field of expertise. By moving into a new area, he severely hurt his credibility, and the judge refused to allow him to testify before the jury.

After the witness acknowledged that for at least the prior 15-20 years, he had not performed a physical examination of a single child alleged to have been sexually abused, this exchange about the use of the colposcope occurred:

Question: Okay, so we have an idea to decide what weight to put on your opinions, you don't recall doing any exams, if you . . . have done them, at least twenty years ago or fifteen years ago?
Answer: Yes. Correct.
Question: You have never used a colposcope?
Answer: Correct.
Question: Have never seen, personally, a colposcope, I gather.
Answer: Correct.
Question: You have never done any research yourself into the area that you've just talked about of vaginal openings of young girls.
Answer: Well, I have not myself been conducting examinations.
. . .
Question: You have not conducted a research project with children as a subject?
Answer: That's correct.

SOURCE: Testimony of proposed defense expert witness in *State v. Werlein* (*November 7, 1989*).

instantly make him or her an expert in all related areas. The expert witness who strays from his or her true area of expertise will be humbled and likely humiliated quickly.

❑ **Locating the Expert Witness**

Expert witnesses generally come into a case in one of two ways. Most frequently, the individual has been involved in the case factually and, because of his or her special training and expertise, is able also to testify as an expert witness—a doctor who examined a patient or a therapist who worked with a victim, for example.

In other situations, attorneys might specifically seek out individuals to testify as experts. These would be professionals who have had no prior involvement with particular cases but are able to offer general background information, opinions, or interpretations about specific facts.

An expert witness might be asked to provide general background information to the jury about an area of specialized knowledge, for example, in a case where a child victim of sexual abuse recanted earlier allegations. Alternatively, an expert might be provided various documents to review and be asked to offer opinions from the materials presented. In such a "paper case," of course, the attorney must provide *all* the available information to the expert. An outside expert witness might also be hired to counter the opinions or conclusions offered by an expert witness presented by the opposing party.

When an attorney needs the testimony of a previously uninvolved expert, where does he or she find one? An initial step should be for the attorney to look within the local community. Each community has its own experts in various professions. Local therapists, doctors, social workers, teachers, scientists, psychologists, and so on are likely to have the knowledge and skills to help educate a jury on issues of interpersonal violence. Local university and teaching hospitals may also provide access to good expert witnesses.

It is important for professionals within the community to be supportive of each other. Those with special knowledge and experience concerning issues of interpersonal violence should be willing to assist local attorneys and law enforcement agencies.

Many communities have well-established networks of professionals. In some areas this involves multidisciplinary teams, whereas in others, informal arrangements exist for interested members within the local professional community to meet regularly to discuss issues

of common concern. These meetings may, for example, include problem solving and provide ongoing training. (Readers who live and
work in communities that do not have some type of cooperative
system should consider this a recommendation to create one.) Those
who participate in these activities are likely to be recognized as the
local experts and might be available to assist in court cases.

Attorneys should be resourceful in seeking to discover local experts. For example, in a child assault case where the injuries are
severe and have been photographically documented, a prosecutor
may consider using the county medical examiner as an "outside"
expert to discuss the probable causes of the injuries (see, e.g., *State v.
Brown*, 1990). In explaining DNA technology, an area hospital-based
researcher can be very helpful (see, e.g., *State v. Cauthron*, 1993). Too
often, attorneys overlook exceptionally qualified experts simply because they are "too close." Additionally, as a tactical matter, attorneys
sometimes believe that the aura of the expert witness is enhanced
when he or she is brought in from out of state—this is the "the further
they travel, the more expert they must be" syndrome.

On the other hand, the attorney can err by refusing to look for an
expert witness outside of the local community. The most knowledgeable expert witness on a particular subject might not be based locally.
It is often desirable to engage the services of the best expert witness
available, and the attorney should be willing to look nationwide for
the professional who can best help advance the case.

The attorney needing an independent expert witness should actively search for a qualified professional. He or she should consult
with colleagues and inquire of local professionals who *they* consider
to be the leading experts in the field. The attorney should determine
what experts other attorneys have used in similar cases, and how
effective these witnesses have been in court. The attorney should not
hesitate to telephone the authors of leading articles and textbooks
and seek their consultation and recommendations. Many of the
professionals who publish articles are also willing to serve as expert
witnesses in court cases. The lawyer should also consider those who
lecture at significant professional conferences.

In deciding which expert to retain as a witness, the lawyer should
consider several factors. The ideal choice will be a well-regarded
professional with excellent credentials. In addition, the witness

should be articulate, personable, and skilled at communicating to laypersons; he or she should be both researcher and active practitioner and should have some courtroom experience, but not so much that he or she is assailable as being a professional witness. Of course, the ideal witness choice would also be someone willing to accept fees that are within existing fiscal constraints (see Chapter 6 for discussion of the setting of fees by expert witnesses). The attorney should be certain to obtain sufficient information to make informed decisions about each of these factors.

In deciding whether to retain an expert witness who is local or from outside the area, several factors might appropriately be considered. Using local experts offers several advantages:

- They are likely to be known and respected by the judges.
- They are likely to be familiar with local court practices and procedures, which can help prevent problems of miscommunication in court.
- The convenience of being able to meet and/or consult with the witness frequently is enhanced when the witness works or lives nearby.
- The witness's proximity to the courthouse allows for greater ease of scheduling and is likely to result in lower costs incurred in witness fees and travel expenses.

In seeking an expert witness in a particular field, the attorney might need to search for someone with specific experience. Many professional organizations are willing to refer attorneys to individuals who might be particularly well qualified to be expert witnesses in court cases. Several professional organizations also maintain speakers' bureaus, which might be good referral starting points. The following are some organizations that attorneys may find useful to contact when seeking expert witnesses:

- American Academy of Pediatrics
141 Northwest Point Boulevard
P.O. Box 927
Elk Grove Village, IL 60009-0927
phone: (708) 228-5005

- American Association for the Advancement of Science
  1333 H Street N.W.
  Washington, DC 20005
  phone: (202) 326-6500

- American Bar Association Center on Children and the Law
  (provides resources and technical assistance for professionals using the legal system)
  740 Fifteenth Street N.W.
  Washington, DC 20005
  phone: (202) 662-1720

- American College of Forensic Psychology
  26701 Quail Creek, No. 295
  Laguna Hills, CA 92656
  phone: (714) 831-0236

- American Medical Association
  Department of Mental Health
  515 N. State
  Chicago, IL 60610
  phone: (312) 464-5000

- American Professional Society on the Abuse of Children
  (the leading multidisciplinary professional organization dealing with issues affecting child abuse and neglect; also has state chapters in at least 40 states)
  407 S. Dearborn, Suite 1300
  Chicago, IL 60605
  phone: (312) 554-0166

- American Prosecutors Research Institute
  (provides support and technical assistance to prosecutors; has several divisions, including the National Center for the Prosecution of Child Abuse, the DNA Legal Assistance Unit, the National Traffic Law Center, and the National Drug Prosecution Center)
  99 Canal Center Plaza, Suite 510
  Alexandria, VA 22314
  phone: (703) 739-0321

- American Psychological Association
  750 First Street N.E.
  Washington, DC 20002
  phone: (202) 336-5500

- Association for the Treatment of Sexual Abusers
  (provides information on issues concerning evaluation and treatment of sexual offenders)
  10700 Southwest Beaverton-Hillsdale Highway, Suite 26
  Beaverton, OR 97005
  phone: (503) 643-1023

- National Association of Social Workers
  750 First Street N.E.
  Washington, DC 20002
  phone: (800) 638-8799

- National Medical Association
  1012 Tenth Street N.W.
  Washington, DC 20001
  phone: (202) 347-1895

- National Resource Center on Child Sexual Abuse
  106 Lincoln Street
  Huntsville, AL 35801
  phone: (205) 533-5437

- People of Color Leadership Institute
  714 G Street S.E.
  Washington, DC 20003
  phone: (202) 544-3144

There are also a number of publications that print lists of expert witnesses (e.g., see Wecht, 1993). Many state bar associations and state trial lawyer associations publish resources such as *The Expert Witness and Litigation Support Handbook,* which include a compilation of expert witnesses who have appeared in the courts of that state. Prosecuting attorneys may also find similar resources within their state prosecutors' associations.

❏ **The Role of a Consulting Expert**

Experts will sometimes be retained by parties involved in litigation to serve as advisers, but not to be witnesses. In such circumstances the professional is referred to as a *consulting* expert as opposed to a *testimonial* expert. The role of the consulting expert entails significantly different expectations and demands on the professional compared with the role of the testimonial expert (see Chapter 6 for further discussion of how the two roles differ).

The consulting expert is retained not to give evidence, but to provide help privately to one party in advocating his or her position. Consulting experts often take a direct, hands-on role in the preparation and presentation of cases. A consultant may be expected to provide background information to the attorney that will help the lawyer understand technical aspects of the evidence. For example, in a case relying upon DNA identification evidence, an attorney might hire a molecular biologist solely to educate him or her about the science involved; an attorney might retain a psychologist for consultation in a case involving complex issues of mental illness.

Consulting experts often do more than merely educate attorneys; they are frequently substantially involved in the handling of cases. A consulting expert may be asked to provide technical guidance, conduct a literature review, critique opposing experts' reports, advise the attorney on strategy, prepare trial exhibits, draft questions for direct examination, and actively participate in the preparation of the cross-examination of the opposing expert.

When an expert witness is providing testimony, he or she owes a special obligation of candor to the court. In that role, the testimonial expert witness is ethically bound, for example, to acknowledge the limitations of his or her own opinions and to refrain from overstating the literature. A consulting expert's obligation, in contrast, is to the attorney who has retained his or her services. This key distinction allows the consulting expert to provide advocacy in lieu of professional objectivity and balance.

As a consultant, a professional can appropriately help to identify and exploit weaknesses in the views and work of the opposing side. Consider, for example, the role of a consulting expert in a child sexual abuse case in which a medical doctor is expected to testify for the plaintiff that the child victim's medical findings are consistent with sexual abuse. The retained consultant might not disagree, ultimately, with the conclusions drawn by the examining doctor, but in the role of consultant, he or she will be asked to assist in the refuting of that evidence.

The consulting expert should anticipate that he or she will be asked to assist the attorney in critiquing the manner and method of the examination process, the reliability of the supporting research, the validity of that research, perhaps even the competence of the examining doctor. The consultant may be asked to provide contrary research articles and alternative explanations for the findings reported.

The consulting expert might be retained to sit with the attorney at counsel table during the opposing doctor's testimony in order to provide instant feedback and input into the cross-examination. In this scenario, the hired expert is asked to advise the attorney on the weaknesses of the position of the examining doctor's opinion, even though if the consultant were required to testify he or she might be unable to disagree intellectually with the examining doctor's ultimate conclusions. Accordingly, the expert serves only as an adviser, and does not testify at the trial.

Sometimes one party will retain a particular expert merely to make that person unavailable as a witness for the other side (see the discussion in Chapter 6).

An expert hired as a consultant should be paid an hourly rate or a set consultation fee. A consultant should never be compensated based upon a contingency fee arrangement whereby his or her earnings are dependent upon the outcome of the trial.

❏ Court-Appointed Experts

The rules of evidence permit the court to appoint its own expert witnesses:

> The court may on its own motion or on the motion of any party enter an order to show cause why expert witnesses should not be appointed, and may request the parties to submit nominations. The court may

appoint any expert witness agreed to by the parties, and may appoint expert witnesses of its own selection. Any expert witness shall not be appointed by the court unless the witness consents to act. A witness so appointed shall be informed of the witness's duties by the court in writing, a copy of which shall be filed with the clerk, or at a conference in which the parties shall have opportunity to participate. A witness so appointed shall advise the parties of the witness's findings, if any; the witness's deposition may be taken by any party; and the witness may be called to testify by the court or any party. The witness shall be subject to cross examination by each party, including a party calling the witness. (Federal Rules of Evidence 706[a])

As one court observed, "A court expert serves not only as a witness on whose opinion the court can rely for assistance, but also as both a second set of ears for the court and a teacher who, unaffected by his having been called as a witness by one side or the other, can explain the technical significance of the evidence presented" (*Leesona Corp. v. Varta Batteries, Inc.*, 1981).

Traditionally, court-appointed experts have been used infrequently. There is a long-standing debate about the merits of using court-appointed expert witnesses.[4] It has been suggested that the use of an independent, well-informed, well-respected expert who is permitted to testify without any allegiance to a specific client can enhance the ability of the fact finder to ascertain the truth and to distinguish accuracy from advocacy. The problem, and much of the controversy, arises from the issue of whether any truly informed, independent, and perfectly objective experts can be found.

If a court-appointed expert is not current in the literature or is otherwise deficient in knowledge or skill, the court can be grossly misled by that person's testimony. Alternatively, if the supposed "independent" expert is, in fact, a camouflaged partisan on the issue, then the jury will receive an opinion from a witness who is given a special aura of infallibility, without the recognition that the witness holds a particular bias. In either case, the danger is that the court-selected expert can be given too much deference. If that expert is not wisely chosen, then the risk of an injustice may be enhanced.

❏ Notes

1. This is clearly the majority rule in the United States. The rule discussed here has been increasingly criticized, however. Perhaps no criticism has been as pointed, or as articulate, as that of Judge Higginbotham in *In Re Air Crash Disaster at New Orleans, LA* (1986).

2. The witness was Dr. Judith Becker.

3. This is an excerpt from the trial testimony of Dr. Carol Baer in *State v. Owens* (1996).

4. For arguments advocating the use of court experts, see, for example, Griffin (1961); for arguments against the use of court-appointed experts, see Levy (1961) and De Parcq (1956).

3

The Preparation of Expert Witness Testimony

To have any chance at all of pulling a rabbit out of a hat in a trial, you have to come to court armed with 50 rabbits, 50 hats and a lot of luck.

Edward Bennett Williams[1]

The key to the effective presentation of expert testimony is effective preparation. The failure to prepare adequately for expert testimony can result in critical information being kept from the jury. When that occurs, an accurate determination of truth is jeopardized.

Every witness, no matter how smart or experienced, can improve his or her courtroom testimony through efficient pretrial preparation with the attorney who will present the testimony. Every attorney, no matter how skilled or experienced, can improve the presentation of an expert witness's testimony through intelligent pretrial preparation with the witness. This chapter discusses how the attorney and the expert witness can most effectively prepare the presentation of expert testimony.

❏ What an Attorney Must Do to Prepare Expert Witness Testimony

Before an attorney can prepare an expert witness to testify, the attorney must first prepare him- or herself. If the expert witness's primary job is to teach, then the attorney's primary job is to learn. Preparation of expert testimony should begin with the attorney's careful analysis of exactly *why* he or she is seeking to present the expert testimony. At the outset, the attorney should consider these questions:

- What does the attorney hope to accomplish by presenting expert witness testimony?[2]
- What point does the attorney need the expert to teach to the judge or jury?
- Is expert witness testimony really needed?
- What is the expert going to be able to say that no other witness can say? Is there really no other, or better, way to present this information to the jury?
- What problems will be solved through the use of expert testimony?
- What problems will be created by the use of expert testimony?
- Will the presentation of expert testimony result in the opposing side calling its own expert witness, thus leading to an unnecessary "battle of the experts"?
- Will the expert testimony invite unnecessary evidentiary rulings and risk injecting potential, yet avoidable, error on appeal?

The attorney should thoroughly consider the issues raised by these questions in order to make informed decisions regarding whether and how to use expert witness testimony. This analysis will also help him or her to determine more precisely the scope of any testimony (see also the discussion in Chapter 1).

Careful consideration of these issues is also vital in establishing the exact role for the expert witness. For the witness and the lawyer to work in ideal concert, the expert witness's role must be specifically defined. The expert witness must understand what is expected of him or her; he or she can most effectively provide assistance only when it is clear precisely what he or she is being asked to do. That cannot be articulated by the attorney until the attorney determines exactly what he or she seeks to accomplish by using the expert witness.

A careful evaluation of why the expert witness is being asked to testify involves several important considerations. It demands that the attorney understand clearly all that the expert witness can and cannot say. It forces the attorney to consider whether *this* expert is really the proper expert for the particular case. Further, it requires that the attorney know exactly what the legal limitations of expert witness testimony are in his or her particular jurisdiction.

WHAT THE EXPERT CAN AND CANNOT SAY, SCIENTIFICALLY

The lawyer must be fully aware of what the expert witness can and cannot say based upon the state of the scientific literature. This requires the lawyer to be knowledgeable about the expert's field of practice. The lawyer cannot properly elicit information without knowing what information there is to be elicited.

The attorney's understanding of the scientific limitations of the expert witness's testimony will also help ensure that he or she does not hold false expectations for the scope of that testimony. Additionally, this knowledge will allow the attorney to be more certain that the evidence he or she seeks to introduce will be truly beneficial to the case. For example, in a criminal child sexual abuse case a prosecutor might expect a conviction based on the belief that he or she can call a medical expert who will testify that sexual abuse occurred. The prosecutor may believe that certain medical findings made during the genital examination of a child will *prove* that the child suffered penetrating injury. The existing literature, however, might establish that such injuries are not definite proof of abuse, but are only indicative of "possible abuse" (see Adams, 1993). The witness will be unable to testify as the prosecutor might anticipate.

Alternatively, a lawyer might believe that the definitive proof of identity of the defendant in a rape case will be the forensic scientist's testimony of a "match" between head hairs found at the rape scene and head hairs taken from the defendant. The lawyer should discover *pretrial* that the forensic scientist will not testify that this means the head hairs from the crime scene came from the defendant, but will merely state that the hairs show "microscopic similarities such that they *could have* come from the same source." That might not be exactly what the attorney was anticipating.

Before the expert witness testifies, therefore, the lawyer must do some homework. He or she must become familiar with the expert witness's field of practice, by reading the leading literature, reviewing the significant research, learning the vocabulary, and gaining some understanding of the basic principles and theories. To present expert testimony most effectively, the lawyer should know what the expert knows, why the expert knows it, and how the expert is going to articulate it.

In court, the lawyer must be able to carry on an informed and instructive dialogue with the expert witness, in a manner simple enough for the jury to understand. The lawyer must guide the expert witness to teach the jury. To be an effective guide, one must know the territory.

STUDYING THE LITERATURE

To present expert testimony effectively, the attorney must know the literature in the expert's field of practice. The lawyer has an affirmative obligation to locate and study that material; if the lawyer does not become familiar with the material, he or she cannot properly present expert testimony.

The expert witness has an important role in the education of the attorney. The attorney should expect the expert to help provide the necessary background information and to be willing to teach the attorney enough of what he or she knows so that the attorney can most efficiently elicit the expert's testimony in court. The expert should be willing to explain the basic principles of his or her field of practice and should also be prepared to provide to the lawyer the leading articles in his or her field. The expert should also be available to answer technical questions from the lawyer throughout the pretrial period.

The lawyer, however, should not wait until the first meeting with the expert witness to begin his or her education process. Skilled trial lawyers begin studying the expert's field on their own. The attorney can and should begin to study the relevant literature early in the process of preparing for trial. Every field has two or three leading articles. The attorney should consult with colleagues and authorities in the particular field involved in the litigation to identify these principal articles, and then should obtain and read them.

> *Skilled trial lawyers begin studying the expert's field on their own.*

Most of the scholarly articles the attorney will need are available at university libraries. Librarians can help identify and locate important articles in specific fields. Some of this information may also be available through on-line computer information services. Attorneys whose practices regularly include cases in particular fields should consider belonging to professional organizations that provide relevant journals and other resource material. For example, a child abuse prosecutor or guardian *ad litem* might want to belong to the American Professional Society on the Abuse of Children to obtain its publications, the *APSAC Advisor* and *Child Maltreatment*.[3]

What the attorney is looking for in studying the basic literature is a very general understanding of the field. The attorney needs to know at least these things:

- What are the basic principles and theories in this field?
- What concepts influence the expert's thinking?
- What information does the expert use to make decisions? What process?
- What methodology does the expert use to draw conclusions?
- What facts will an expert need to know to render an opinion?
- What significant things are known to the experts in this field that might not be known to the layperson/juror?
- Does the research report findings that are different from what a layperson might expect?
- What are the limitations of this field of science?
- Does the research lead the attorney to discover additional facts about the case that might be important?
- What are the "terms of art" in the particular field?

A Bibliography for Lawyers:
Some Recommended Readings
in the Field of Interpersonal Violence

Effects of Sexual Abuse

Conte, J., & Schuerman, J. (1987). The effects of sexual abuse on children. *Journal of Interpersonal Violence, 2,* 380-390.

Friedrich, W. N. (1993). Sexual victimization and sexual behavior in children: A review of recent literature. *Child Abuse and Neglect, 17,* 59-66.

Kendall-Tackett, K. A., Williams, L. M., & Finkelhor, D. (1993). Impact of sexual abuse on children: A review and synthesis of recent empirical studies. *Psychological Bulletin, 113,* 164-180.

Delayed Reporting of Child Sexual Abuse

Lawson, L., & Chaffin, M. (1992). False negatives in sexual abuse disclosure interviews. *Journal of Interpersonal Violence, 7,* 532-542.

Sorenson, T., & Snow, B. (1991). How children tell: The process of disclosure in child sexual abuse. *Child Welfare, 70,* 3-15.

Recantation of Sexual Abuse Allegations

Summit, R. (1983). The child sexual abuse accommodation syndrome. *Child Abuse and Neglect, 7,* 177-193.

Summit, R. (1992). Abuse of the child sexual abuse accommodation syndrome. *Journal of Child Sexual Abuse, 1*(4), 153-163.

Reliability of Allegations of Sexual Abuse

Everson, M., & Boat, B. (1989). False accusations of sexual abuse by children and adolescents. *Journal of the American Academy of Child and Adolescent Psychiatry, 28,* 230-235.

Jones, D. P. H., & McGraw, J. M. (1987). Reliable and fictitious accounts of sexual abuse to children. *Journal of Interpersonal Violence, 2,* 27-45.

Thoennes, N., & Tjaden, P. G. (1990). The extent, nature and validity of sexual abuse allegations in custody/visitation disputes. *Child Abuse and Neglect, 14,* 151-163.

Suggestibility of Children and Children's Memory

Ceci, S. J., & Bruck, M. (1995). *Jeopardy in the courtroom.* Hyattsville, MD: American Psychological Association.

Lyon, T. D. (1985). False allegations and false denials in child sexual abuse. *Journal of Psychology, Public Policy and Law, 1*(2), 429.

Reed, L. D. (1996). Findings from research on children's suggestibility and implications for conducting child interviews. *Child Maltreatment, 1,* 105-120.

Saywitz, K. J. (1995). Improving children's testimony: The question, the answer, and the environment. In M. S. Zaragoza, J. R. Graham, G. C. N. Hall, R. Hirschman, & Y. S. Ben-Porath (Eds.), *Memory and testimony in the child witness* (pp. 113-140). Thousand Oaks, CA: Sage.

(Continued)

Saywitz, K. J., & Goodman, G. S. (1996). Interviewing children in and out of court: Current research and practice implications. In J. Briere, L. Berliner, J. A. Bulkley, C. Jenny, & T. Reid (Eds.), *The APSAC handbook on child maltreatment* (pp. 297-318). Thousand Oaks, CA: Sage.

Saywitz, K. J., Goodman, G. S., & Myers, J. E. B. (1990). Can children provide accurate eyewitness reports? *Violence Update, 1*(1), 3-9.

Whitcomb, D., Runyan, D. K., De Vos, E., Hunter, W. M., Cross, T. P., Everson, M. D., Peeler, N. A., Porter, C. Q., Toth, P. A., & Cropper, C. (1992). *Final report* (Child Victim as Witness Research and Development Program, Grant No. 87-MC-CX-0026, National Institute of Justice). Boston: Education Development Center.

Medical Evidence in Child Sexual Abuse Cases

Adams, J. A. (1993). Classification of anogenital findings in children with suspected sexual abuse: An evolving process. *APSAC Advisor, 6*(2), 11-13.

Adams, J. A., Harper, K., Knudson, S., & Revilla, J. (1994). Examination findings in legally confirmed child sexual abuse: It's normal to be normal. *Pediatrics, 94*, 310-317.

Bays, J., & Chadwick, D. (1993). Medical diagnosis of the sexually abused child, *Child Abuse and Neglect, 17*, 91-110.

Muram, D. (1989). Child sexual abuse: Relationship between sexual acts and genital findings. *Child Abuse and Neglect, 13*, 211-216.

Physical Abuse of Children

Alexander, R. (Ed.). (1994). Child fatalities [Special issue]. *APSAC Advisor, 7*(4).

Kempe, C. H., Silverman, F. N., Steele, B. F., Droegemuller, W., & Silver, A. K. (1962). The battered-child syndrome. *Journal of the American Medical Association, 181*, 17-24.

Reese, R. M. (1994). *Child abuse medical diagnosis and management.* Philadelphia: Lea & Febiger.

Effects of Rape

Burgess, A. W., & Holmstrom, L. L. (1974). Rape trauma syndrome. *American Journal of Psychiatry, 13*, 981-986.

Resick, P. A. (1993). The psychological impact of rape. *Journal of Interpersonal Violence, 8*, 223-255.

Battered Spouse

Walker, L. E. A. (1992). Battered women syndrome and self-defense. *Notre Dame Journal of Law, Ethics and Public Policy, 6*, 321-334.

Use of DNA Evidence to Establish Identity

Lander, E., & Budowle, B. (1994). Commentary: DNA fingerprinting dispute laid to rest. *Nature, 371*, 735-738.

National Research Council. (1992). *DNA technology in forensic science.* Washington, DC: National Academy Press.

National Research Council. (1996). *The evaluation of forensic DNA evidence.* Washington, DC: National Academy Press.

If the attorney studies the principal literature before meeting with the expert witness, the preliminary discussions will be much more productive. The more knowledgeable the attorney, the more exacting the information he or she can obtain from the expert witness. The informed attorney will be better able to ask precise questions of the expert and thus obtain the most useful information. This is particularly important because the information the expert witness provides in the early stages of trial preparation is often helpful in directing the course of further factual investigations.

The lawyer's knowing something about the expert's field will also focus discussions about the merits of the case. This should lead the attorney to a quicker analysis of the strength of his or her case. Such awareness is apt to bring about a sensible and efficient resolution to the case.

Once the attorney has identified a potential expert witness, he or she should ask the expert for specific articles, books, or similar reference materials to study. In particular, the attorney will want to review the source material the expert believes is most relevant in the particular case. Even though the attorney may already have read other articles in the field, it is important that he or she be familiar with the materials the expert witness considers to be important.

Conversely, the attorney should tell the expert which articles he or she has already read. The attorney may believe a particular article is influential and may intend to rely upon it, only to learn that the expert thinks it is based on bad science. Or the attorney may bring to the expert's attention an important article that he or she had missed. At times, the expert can learn from the lawyer.

As a practical consideration, an expert witness is likely to be more motivated to assist an attorney who has already made an obvious effort to learn than one who has not. The expert is likely to respect an attorney who has done his or her homework and can talk intelligently about the subject matter at hand. This can substantially enhance the collegial working relationship between lawyer and expert.

WHAT THE EXPERT CAN
AND CANNOT SAY, LEGALLY

The lawyer must be completely aware of the legal limitations on expert witness testimony. There are likely to be specific *threshold* requirements to the admissibility of expert testimony, and the attorney must know what these foundational requirements are and how to meet them.

The scope of the admissibility of expert testimony varies from jurisdiction to jurisdiction, and often from year to year (see, generally, Myers et al., 1989; see also Myers, 1992). Additionally, the admissibility of novel scientific evidence is governed by specific rules that may have recently changed or may be subject to change (see, e.g., Stern, 1994; see also the discussion in Chapter 1). The attorney must be aware of the precise state of the law in this area.

Specific limitations on the *scope* of the expert's testimony will also exist. The attorney cannot present expert witness testimony in the most effective manner without knowing both the legal requirements and the limitations of such evidence.

There may be certain things the attorney wants to elicit from an expert witness that he or she may discover are not admissible under the rules of evidence. Failing to be aware of this pretrial can lead to the erroneous introduction of evidence, which can result in a mistrial or reversal on appeal.

Similarly, there are likely to be certain things an expert might want to say that the rules of evidence will not permit. It will be the job of the attorney to guide the expert witness through the legal foundational requirements and around restrictions on the expert's testimony. The attorney should explain these restrictions to the expert before he or she testifies, to avoid potential problems in court. For example, in many jurisdictions an expert can discuss characteristics of child sexual abuse victims in general, but may not testify in such a way as to vouch for the credibility of a particular child involved in a specific case. The attorney must know this and advise the expert witness of this limitation during pretrial preparation. Otherwise, the expert may unwittingly testify about things the law does not permit, causing the case to be mistried or resulting in a conviction being reversed.

IS THIS THE PROPER EXPERT WITNESS?

A review of the research, literature, and law might lead the attorney to the conclusion that the intended expert witness will be unable to testify in the manner the attorney had hoped. For instance, the attorney may discover that the expert witness will not be helpful for trial, or may decide that a different type of expert witness is needed in the particular case. An attorney handling a case involving DNA evidence used to establish the identity of the assailant, for example, might expect to rely upon a forensic scientist as the only expert witness in the case. It might be that the attorney is intending to have a molecular biologist discuss the nuances and principles of DNA typing, show that the principles are accepted in the scientific community, and demonstrate the existence of a DNA banding pattern match that establishes a definitive "DNA fingerprint" linking the defendant to the crime scene. Upon reviewing the literature in the field, however, the attorney is likely to discover that the issues of the principles of forensic DNA typing are no longer controverted and are accepted in the scientific community, but that science does not support an absolute "DNA fingerprint." The attorney might learn that in a contested hearing he or she may not need a molecular biologist to establish the *ability* to generate a reliable DNA banding pattern, but might instead need an expert in population genetics to testify about the *meaning* of a DNA banding pattern match.

Similarly, an attorney might believe the best expert witness to discuss medical findings in a child abuse case will be a doctor. It may be, however, that the most informed and experienced professional in the area is not a doctor but a nurse practitioner who performs the sexual abuse examinations at the local child abuse center. For this case, the nurse practitioner, not the doctor, may be the better expert witness to educate the jurors.

MEETING WITH THE EXPERT WITNESS

No witness, especially an expert witness, should ever go into court to testify without first meeting with the attorney who will present the testimony. And no attorney should ever take an expert witness into court to offer expert testimony without first meeting with the expert to discuss the testimony. Allowing an expert witness to testify in court without meeting first with the attorney is like asking a soldier to go into battle without checking to see if his weapon works.

The first meeting between expert witness and attorney should occur in the expert witness's office. This serves the attorney in several ways:

- It ensures that the expert witness will have access to his or her files and notes about the case.
- It allows the attorney to observe the textbooks and other resource materials the expert has in his or her office, and to discover what literature the expert witness most relies upon.
- It affords the attorney the opportunity to obtain copies of specific articles or other resource materials the expert witness has in his or her files. The lawyer should also obtain a copy of the expert's curriculum vitae at this time.
- It permits the attorney to observe the expert witness's office, laboratory, or other working environment. An office visit gives the attorney a fuller context for the work the expert witness performs. For example, if the expert witness is a medical doctor, the attorney can observe the specific equipment used during examinations; if the expert witness is a psychologist, the attorney can learn how his or her office is designed. This can be especially helpful for the attorney's efforts to illustrate for the jury how interactions between the expert witness and other witnesses occurred. If a child witness in a trial testifies, for instance, that in sessions with her therapist there was a zebra in the room, it is useful for the attorney to have been in the therapist's office and seen the stuffed zebra toy in the corner. Such knowledge is also particularly useful to counter points made during cross-examination.
- It affords the attorney the opportunity to look around the expert's office or laboratory for items that can be used as exhibits and teaching aids at trial.
- It demonstrates to the expert witness the attorney's commitment to the case, that he or she is willing to do the traveling to discuss the case.

The initial meeting between expert witness and attorney serves several objectives. As discussed above, one of these is for both parties to understand what the other person expects of them. The attorney's main objective is to be certain he or she understands several things: how the expert witness became involved in the case, what work the expert witness has done on the case, precisely what the expert's opinions are about the case, and how the expert will be able to express those opinions. Similarly, the expert witness's objective should be to clarify what his or her role is going to be in the trial.

Attorney and expert should begin an open exchange of information and education at their first meeting. The lawyer should review all the material the witness has accumulated concerning the case (for a discussion of client privilege issues, see Chapter 6) and should determine what additional information the expert might need. The lawyer should also be sure to learn *why* the expert wants any additional information.

> *Attorney and expert should begin an open exchange of information and education at their first meeting.*

The attorney should tell the expert what reading he or she has already done and seek guidance on other technical materials and articles to review. In particular, the lawyer should obtain from the expert those materials the expert believes are most influential in the field and those the expert intends to rely upon in his or her testimony. This initial meeting will provide direction for the attorney and the witness as well as mutual education, so both can perform their jobs better.

The attorney should provide the expert witness with enough information so that the expert understands the basic theories of the case. The lawyer must not be shy about soliciting the expert's suggestions about how he or she can best assist. The attorney can enhance the opportunity to obtain the expert's guidance by asking one specific question at the end of the meeting: "Is there anything else you think I should ask you that I haven't asked, that might be helpful to this case?" In most cases the witness and the lawyer will meet or communicate several times during the pretrial stage, and the lawyer should repeat this question during every one of their discussions. As each gains a better understanding of the role of the other, and lawyer and expert develop a close working relationship, the witness will be able to provide additional helpful information that the lawyer might not think to inquire about.

Throughout the pretrial preparation stage, attorney and expert witness should share additional factual information as they obtain it. Reports from opposing experts may be exchanged and discussed.

The lawyer should feel free to call upon the witness to seek guidance and understanding about the substance and nuances of the professional's field of practice. Similarly, the expert should expect easy access to the attorney. The expert should be able to obtain additional factual materials easily, as well as information about practical issues such as court scheduling.

WHAT DOES AN ATTORNEY ASK AN EXPERT?

The attorney may know what the expert witness knows, but how will that information be most effectively conveyed to the jury? The lawyer should seek input from the expert witness as to what specific questions should be asked during direct examination and how certain questions might best be phrased. These key questions can form the outline of the expert witness's testimony. The attorney should also seek the witness's recommendations on how technical materials can best be presented and explained to the jury.

The expert witness and the lawyer should discuss the exact nature of the witness's testimony before trial. It is the expert's job to provide information to the court; however, it is the lawyer's job to learn what questions will best elicit that information. The lawyer should encourage the witness to propose specific questions to be asked in court that may help trigger effective responses. The lawyer needs to put his or her ego aside and allow the witness to recommend specific questions.

The expert witness comes to court with a wealth of knowledge and information to share. It is the job of the lawyer to determine the most effective way of cuing the expert witness to provide that information. Any help the witness can provide in offering those cues should be gratefully received. This relationship may be compared to a relay race: Before the second runner can start, the first runner must pass the baton. Just as the baton-passing runner should transfer the baton exactly the way the receiver feels most comfortable accepting it, so the attorney should cue the expert in the manner that makes the expert best able to respond.

It may be beneficial for the expert witness to draft specific questions that he or she recommends should be asked during his or her testimony. For example, forensic scientists for the FBI, who frequently travel throughout the country testifying about laboratory work they have done in cases, often greet prosecutors with detailed lists of the questions they should be asked during their testimony. Such recommendations should be welcomed, and not perceived as any slight to the ingenuity or competence of the attorney. These experts have testified many times in court and thus have a wide range of experience. They know precisely what information they have to share and how it can best be provided to the jury. The lawyer should welcome such witnesses' suggested questions and consider them as a guide.

Some expert witnesses who testify frequently may themselves maintain lists of specific questions they have found particularly helpful in eliciting information in court. They should not hesitate to offer such lists to attorneys as assistance. It should be cautioned, however, that the expert goes too far when he or she scripts the direct examination. Prepared questions should be used only as a *guide*. Assistance in key areas is one thing; a prepared, detailed dialogue is another (see the discussion of this topic in Chapter 6).

There are several published sources of introductory or *predicate* questions. For criminal child abuse cases, a prosecutor should consult the National Center for Prosecution of Child Abuse's *Investigation and Prosecution of Child Abuse* (1993). Other sources may include, for example, Ferguson and Fine's *Washington Practice, Criminal Law* (1990, e.g., § 1223, 1915, 2508).

One effective method of pretrial preparation is for the lawyer and the expert witness to role-play, each taking on the in-court role of the other. Thus the expert witness asks questions he or she believes are most helpful to elicit pivotal information, and the lawyer acts as the witness, answering those questions. By asking the questions, the witness demonstrates what will best trigger the responses to guide the testimony; by responding to the expert's questions, the lawyer is able to assess whether he or she has truly mastered the substance of the material.

During pretrial meetings, the expert must be encouraged to discuss the weak spots in his or her testimony. The attorney and the expert witness must work together to attempt to identify the areas where the expert's testimony is most vulnerable. Professionals know the limitations of their conclusions as well as the limitations inherent in their fields. The expert witness must be willing to share those limitations with the attorney pretrial.

The expert witness should *never* try to hide or ignore the weaknesses of his or her work. Instead, he or she should voluntarily highlight specific areas of concern with the attorney before trial. From that discussion, lawyer and expert can develop a plan to combat or respond to those points. This might be accomplished by having the expert take the position of an opposing expert and attempt to critique the existing reports and work performed. Once the weak areas have been identified, the lawyer and the expert should then work together to determine how they can best be addressed. (Of course, if it develops that these weaknesses undermine the expert witness's conclusions, the lawyer must reexamine the merits of proceeding with the theory of the case.)

The lawyer might also invite the expert to review the reports of other expert witnesses in the case (although this is subject to various strategic considerations; see the discussion below as well as Chapter 6). This may provide additional information to the witness that bolsters his or her opinions. Alternatively, it might help identify where the opposing side will seek to attack the expert's opinions.

❏ The Expert Witness's Preparation for Trial

Before testifying in court, the expert witness must be thoroughly prepared to present his or her opinions and defend them. This requires that the expert be completely familiar with the case material and the relevant literature.

The expert witness comes into court with a special aura of authority and credibility. Displaying a lack of familiarity with the subject of his or her testimony will lead to the immediate surrender of that appearance of authority. A commanding opinion is supported by a command of the material. The expert who fails the latter also fails the former.

REVIEW OF ALL MATERIALS

If the witness is going to be asked to give an opinion about the facts of a case, the witness must *know* all the facts of the case. Before trial, the witness should consider what additional information he or she needs to make thorough and professional judgments in the case. If the expert thinks additional material will help him or her in drawing conclusions, he or she should ask the attorney for that material before trial.

In those instances in which the expert witness is involved in a "paper case," reviewing documents supplied by the attorney, steps should be taken to ensure that the expert is provided with all the material necessary to form a comprehensive and defensible opinion. The attorney, of course, should equip the expert with all the information available. If it appears to the expert, however, that he or she has been denied access to complete or requested additional material, the witness should avoid further involvement in the case. The witness must have all the information necessary to draw professional opinions.

KNOWLEDGE OF THE CASE MATERIAL

To be effective as a witness, the expert must be completely familiar with the case file. He or she must know what was done, what was said, who said it, when it was said, and how it meshed with what others said.

The attorney who will present the expert witness's testimony will be expected to have read the expert's report many times. The prepared opposing attorney will have read the reports numerous times. It is likely that both attorneys will have highlighted and outlined certain parts of the expert's report in anticipation of presenting or cross-examining the expert's testimony. The expert witness should assume that the skilled opposing attorney will have the expert's reports organized for his or her attack: Sections might be tabbed or underlined with color-coordinated highlighters, with references to contradictions and literature all scripted out. The skilled cross-examiner is likely to bounce the expert through his or her reports in several different directions, in an intended whirlwind of confusion.

If a pretrial deposition was conducted, the expert should expect the same treatment with the deposition transcript. Accordingly, he or she should thoroughly review that document before trial.

The expert witness must know the case file and what he or she has previously said about this case. The witness should also know what he or she has said about similar cases. In short, the expert witness *must* know the file cold.

The witness needs to read and reread the file. If necessary, it should be rearranged in a way that makes it easy for the witness to access specific documents while testifying. The witness might consider making an outline of critical information, dates, or people in preparation for testifying. The witness is permitted to prepare a summary of the file to assist him or her in giving testimony.

The witness will be permitted to bring the file and/or the summary to the witness stand; however, the witness should be cautious in doing so, because the opposing attorney is likely to be able to review any summary the witness brings to court. If the witness is going to bring the file, a careful review of the file should be made to decide if everything need be brought to court. (For example, letters from the presenting attorney to the witness about the case could be used to assail the witness's credibility. A particularly carelessly worded letter might be used to make the witness look like a "hired gun" for that side.)

Whatever it takes to help the expert know the file should be used. This point cannot be overemphasized: *The expert must know what is in his or her file.* The witness must also give the *appearance* of being intimately familiar with the file. Responding to a question by fumbling through a file with a "I know it's in here somewhere" or a "I think I remember . . . " will make the witness look anything but professional. To be convincing, the witness must sound convincing. That means presenting the material in a calm, confident, and professional manner. The witness can do that only if he or she has fully prepared for trial.

KNOWLEDGE OF THE LITERATURE

The witness does not need to know every article and book written in a particular field. (Discussion of how to deal with questions about articles unfamiliar to the witness appears in Chapter 5.) However, if there are specific, well-known articles that are at the core of the expert witness's opinions, the witness should be very familiar with them. If the witness cites sources in his or her report, then the witness must know that material and know it well.

As noted earlier in this chapter, there are certain articles that are considered to be the leading writings in any field. The expert witness must be familiar with those articles in his or her area of expertise and should carefully review them before giving testimony. Likewise, if the attorney intends to ask the witness about specific articles, he or she should be sure to tell the witness beforehand so the expert can review them carefully pretrial.

It is also wise for the witness to review the latest literature in his or her field to be certain that the articles he or she intends to rely upon have not been recently repudiated or assailed. An updated literature review is a wise precaution for the expert pretrial. There is no such thing as being overprepared to testify.

PREPARATION OF EXHIBITS

We live in a visual, multimedia-oriented era, and attorneys and expert witnesses should utilize the innovations of technology to tell their stories. Courtroom testimony is basically radio communication: two people talking while a group of interested persons listen in. To the extent that the courtroom conversation can become less like radio and more like television, the better the potential for the jurors to follow and understand the testimony. Trial exhibits are very important aids to supplement testimony. Pictures, slides, charts, graphs, illustrations, models, and reenactment demonstrations should be considered to enhance the effective presentation of expert testimony.

In pretrial discussions, both the attorney and the expert witness should explore how best to illustrate the expert's testimony. The expert witness should be encouraged to use visual aids in his or her testimony. The attorney should ask the expert witness what visual aids would benefit his or her presentation of testimony. It is also likely that the expert witness will be asked to help prepare those exhibits by assisting in locating or creating charts, illustrations, models, and other attention-sustaining demonstrative aids.

For example, in a case involving physical injuries to a victim's head, the witness may illustrate the injuries by using a Styrofoam model of a head; large color pictures; a mannequin, doll, or even a stuffed animal; drawings; overhead-projected images; or an actual teaching skull. Specific photographs taken of the victim might be substantially enlarged and used during the testimony. The expert witness should be constantly thinking about what kind of visual aids will be helpful to explain his or her testimony.

Many expert witnesses are teachers. In preparing for trial, a witness might consider what visual aids he or she would use to demonstrate certain points if this were a presentation in a classroom setting. For example, in a child sexual abuse case a doctor testifying about medical findings of abuse may have colposcopic slides of the injured genitalia. There is a better way to educate the jury about the significance of the findings than simply showing them the slides of the injured child, however. Consider the educational impact of the doctor first presenting a slide of a "normal" child's genitals and teaching what they are "supposed to" look like. Then the "normal" slide can be displayed side by side with the slide of the victim. As the doctor shows the injured areas, the jurors, with the doctor's guidance, can compare the two slides. Such a comparison can quickly and compellingly educate the jury as to why the injuries seen are significant (for excellent photographs and discussion of this topic, see Heger & Emans, 1992).

In another situation, if an expert witness is testifying about a particular scientific procedure, he or she might bring into the courtroom the actual tools or equipment used in the laboratory. Instead of only talking about how he or she conducted the procedure, the expert can show the jury.

"Show and tell" was a great concept in second grade, and it's a great concept in a courtroom as well. The expert witness should be encouraged to be as creative and innovative as possible in considering the preparation of illustrative trial exhibits.

CONSULTATION WITH OTHER EXPERTS

As a general rule, an expert witness is entitled to testify based upon any information he or she has considered, so long as it is "of a type reasonably relied upon by experts in the particular field in forming opinions or inferences upon the subject" (Federal Rules of Evidence

An Attorney's Discovery—
and the Ideal Expert

A lawyer was trying one of the early cases using DNA technology to establish the identification of the defendant in a serial rape case. He knew nothing about science, and yet needed to conduct an exhaustive pretrial *Frye* hearing. Issues of population genetics were to be at the heart of the hearing.

The expert witnesses had provided volumes of scientific articles delving into the nuances of Hardy-Weinberg equilibrium, linkage equilibrium, and population substructuring. The articles discussed genotypes and mutation rates and allelic frequencies with a vocabulary that only an advanced Ph.D. could appreciate.

Working on the weekend, the lawyer read and reread the articles and consulted his homemade scientific dictionary for hour after hour until he finally thought he understood the point the research scientists were making. Elated, he reflexively reached for the phone to call the expert to confirm his discovery. "I think I understand this," he excitedly offered into the telephone. "I think I understand what these articles say. Let me run it past you, and you tell me if I'm right."

Patiently, politely, the expert allowed the lawyer to review the articles. She congratulated him on his understanding and corrected him on the points missed. Throughout the discussion, it was clear the scientist shared the attorney's excitement of discovery. It was only after about a half hour of this shared discovery that the expert suggested that although she was pleased with the lawyer's breakthrough and amused by his excitement, it might not be a bad idea if he also remembered there was a 3-hour time difference between their homes. "I know you're working hard on this and I'm delighted you are so excited by your understanding of it," she gently told him, "and I appreciate that you are working late into a Saturday evening. But it is 2:30 in the morning here now. Do you think maybe we could discuss this sometime tomorrow instead?"

703). This rule specifically permits the expert to rely upon information even if it might otherwise not be admissible as evidence. This rule of law provides excellent opportunities for the expert witness and the lawyer.

If the expert witness can identify specific individuals he or she considers to be highly respected authorities in the professional field, he or she might consult with those individuals about the case. If the input and opinions of those authorities are "reasonably relied upon" by the expert, the witness may be able to share that information in court. This allows the attorney to introduce into evidence the opinions of renowned authorities, without having to call those persons as witnesses. For example, Dr. Smith is to testify as an expert witness in a criminal case for the state. He is going to offer a specific opinion about a fact in issue that is controverted. Dr. Smith asserts that Dr. Green is the world's leading authority on that particular subject. If Dr. Smith telephones Dr. Green and discusses the case with her, Dr. Smith may be able to testify about that in court (see Chapter 4 for examples of how such testimony would be presented).

During pretrial discussions, therefore, the lawyer might inquire of the expert witness if there are specific leading authorities whose opinions he or she would greatly respect. If so, it might be beneficial for the lawyer to encourage communication between the two experts. Of course, if the authority consulted disagrees with the witness, that probably must be disclosed to the opposing side.[4]

This same analysis holds for documents and other information that is not otherwise admissible. If the expert reasonably relies upon materials outside the record to form his or her opinion, the witness may be able to discuss that information during his or her testimony.

TESTIMONY STARTS WHEN
THE WITNESS APPROACHES THE COURTHOUSE

The expert witness should be aware that jurors may be anywhere around the courthouse when the witness arrives. The woman in line at the coffee shop or the man holding the door open could be a member of the jury. The witness should consider everyone he or she comes into contact with as a potential juror. This means that the witness should not joke about the case, make inappropriate or self-

Bringing the Laboratory Into the Courtroom

It was the first DNA case tried in that jurisdiction. The science was completely foreign to both laypersons and judges.

The molecular biologist who conducted the DNA tests was to testify as an expert witness. She was going to need to explain the intricacies of the DNA identification procedures so that a judge and jury could comprehend exactly how the process worked. Although the scientist was skilled at explaining the process clearly and in simple terminology, it was unavoidable that the instruments involved still sounded complex: a centrifuge, pipettes, electrophoresis, agarose gels, nylon membrane.

To explain the process fully, the attorney asked the witness to take color slides of every piece of equipment in her laboratory. Additionally, she was requested to bring into court with her any small, disposal items used. Meanwhile, the attorney located many of the larger items used by the scientist's laboratory in a local high school science class, and was allowed to borrow them for court.

When the witness testified, every piece of equipment was either in court or displayed there using color slides. When the witness talked about an instrument, the judge and jury either saw it or saw a large picture of it. This process helped demystify the terminology and the process and allowed the judge and jury to understand fully that the procedure involved was not as complicated as they might otherwise have believed.

effacing comments, or act irresponsibly when in or near the courthouse facility.

Similarly, the witness should attempt to prevent other people from making comments about the case in open areas. A good-natured, "Oh, are you here again, Bob?" directed toward the expert witness could be overheard by a juror and interpreted as meaning this witness is a professional for-hire witness. A self-effacing comment such as "I'm here to testify in the *Matthews* case, like I know something about delayed disclosure" may be overheard by a juror who does not recognize the attempt at humility. As soon as the witness comes within a few miles of the courthouse, he or she should take care to behave as if testifying. The expert witness should consider that his or her every word and action may be observed and evaluated by the jury.

PREPARATION CONTINUES
EVEN AFTER THE WITNESS TESTIFIES

Effective trial preparation continues even after the witness has finished testifying. At the end of the trial, the expert witness should debrief with the attorney. The witness and the attorney should discuss what went well and what went poorly. They should also discuss what was overlooked and what questions were not asked that could have gotten more out of the expert witness's testimony.

The witness should also consider debriefing with the court staff and court reporter. These court professionals hear testimony all day and are uniquely situated to give practical and wise advice.[5]

Further, the witness should reflect on the points raised in his or her cross-examination; this experience can be used as a form of education. The expert should be professional enough to consider the criticisms of the opposing attorney; just because an attorney is antagonistic and on the other side does not mean that he or she is wrong. Perhaps the witness will decide to alter certain protocols, note-taking practices, and so on. However, the witness should be careful not to be too self-critical; the mere fact that something has been criticized does not mean the witness was wrong. Each time the expert witness testifies, he or she should learn something that will make him or her a better witness next time.

❏ **Notes**

1. As quoted in Bailey (1985, p. 79).

2. There are advantages and drawbacks to using expert testimony (see the discussion in Chapter 1). Deciding whether to use expert witness testimony is a

complex issue. This is one of those instances when the attorney might be well-advised to consider one of my basic rules of trial practice: Just because you can, doesn't mean you should.

3. APSAC is located at 407 South Dearborn, Suite 1300, Chicago, IL 60605; phone (312) 554-0166.

4. Discovery rules vary greatly from jurisdiction to jurisdiction. In addition, they are often substantially different depending upon the type of litigation involved; criminal rules of discovery are frequently much different from civil rules. In criminal cases, the rules of discovery that apply to the prosecution are often different from those that apply to the defense. The attorney should carefully review the applicable discovery rules governing the particular litigation involved.

5. Although I have been fortunate to learn from some great trial attorneys with whom I have worked, some of the best trial skills advice I have received came from the security guard in a Bridgeton, New Jersey, courtroom. Thanks, Benny.

4

Presenting Expert Testimony in Court

Expert opinion . . . is only an ordinary guess in evening clothes.

Justice Curtis Bok,
Earl M. Kerstetter, Inc., v. Commonwealth, 1961

Performing professional work, being aware of the state of the art and the existing literature, and engaging in a comprehensive preparation of testimony are all mandatory for the most effective presentation of expert testimony in court. However, these things alone are not enough. All of the preparatory work of attorney and expert witness can be wasted if the information gathered and the opinions reached are not explained to the jury in a logical and understandable manner.

When important information is hidden in technical jargon, it is unusable. When evidence is not presented logically, it is of limited benefit. When key pieces of information are not provided to the jury because important questions are not asked, the expert's full value has been squandered.

"And now I'd like to bring on a brand-new witness, with the brightest testimony you're likely to hear for quite some time. She's never been on the stand before, so let's give her a big, warm welcome."

Drawing by Maslin © 1981. The New Yorker Magazine, Inc.

The expert witness and the attorney presenting his or her testimony are most effective when they are in sync. The attorney must know what information the expert witness has to share and then, by asking questions, must cue the witness to share it. The expert witness must be able to explain the information logically, understandably, and credibly. This chapter offers suggestions on how the attorney and the expert witness can most effectively present expert testimony.

❑ The Fear Factor

When the expert witness is called to the stand, both the witness and the attorney generally panic a little. For the expert witness, one fear is that he or she will say something wrong and all the lawyers will jump up and start carrying on, screaming and shaking fingers in his or her general direction. For the attorney, the fear is that the brilliant explanations the witness has provided during pretrial discussions are words the lawyer will never hear again. The attorney also worries that the witness will fall easy prey to the opposing attorney's cross-examination, perhaps even before the third question is asked.

If both the witness and the lawyer understand what is expected of them, they can set these fears aside. This requires an understanding of why the witness is in court and what is being asked of her or him. To be an expert witness requires effective preparation, and, as I will discuss below, skill in providing technical information to the jury.

The expert witness needs specific skills to present expert testimony to a jury effectively. The effective expert witness (a) knows his or her field of practice very well, (b) can explain technical concepts in an understandable manner, (c) appears credible, and (d) is prepared. The best results are achieved when the expert has stayed current in his or her field of professional practice and has performed his or her work to the highest professional and ethical standards. Being an effective expert witness, however, requires more than just being smart.

The presentation of effective testimony involves good teaching skills, but it is also more complex than that: The "students" in a courtroom are laypersons who are not able to ask questions or seek clarification. Their ability to learn is dependent upon the ability of the attorney to ask the right questions and the witness to provide easy-to-understand answers. The expert witness must answer the questions the jurors would ask if they could. The jurors must be taught what they need to know, but the jurors do not get to tell anyone what they need to know.

The expert witness must teach in a personally credible fashion. The jury must not only understand the witness's answers, but must trust the person providing them. In some cases it is more important that the jury trust the expert witness than completely comprehend everything he or she says.

Traditional teaching does not typically involve the rigors of cross-examination. In court, the "teacher" is confronted by an attorney who attempts to discredit the teacher's opinions, methods, knowledge, and, sometimes, ethics. Such is teaching within the adversarial system.

Considerations for the Attorney Presenting Expert Testimony

The best courtroom testimony is nothing more than an interesting conversation overheard. It should be the attorney and the witness engaged in an educational, seemingly spontaneous dialogue that just happens to be taking place in front of the jury. Of course, as with a good play, it takes great preparation to ad-lib that well.

It is not enough for the attorney simply to hire an expert and expect that the expert will teach the jury. The attorney must be the guide for the expert's testimony. The expert witness comes into a case with a tremendous wealth of knowledge; it is the attorney's challenge to discover that knowledge and share it with the jury.

> *The best courtroom testimony is nothing more than an interesting conversation overheard.*

The attorney who fails to do his or her homework fails to realize just how much information an expert witness can bring into the courtroom. In that event the jurors will not be as informed as they can be. That lack of information is what usually causes adverse (and avoidable) verdicts. The lawyer's greatest misuse of an expert witness is the failure to elicit all the information the witness can share with the jury. If the expert witness's knowledge could be measured as a bucket full of water, then the lawyer's task would be to drain every drop of water from that bucket.

An attorney cannot present expert testimony in the most effective manner without knowing what the expert witness knows. The lawyer needs to know the vocabulary and the literature of the expert's field. The attorney must also have an appreciation for the limitations of what the expert witness can and cannot say in court. Of course, the lawyer must also know precisely what work the expert witness has performed in the particular case. With this knowledge, the trial lawyer can begin to determine how to use the expert witness most effectively to educate the jury.

Knowledge alone, however, is not enough. The attorney must also be able to engage the expert witness to present the material clearly and in lay terms. The goal for the attorney should be to elicit information using the expert's knowledge, but to communicate it at a level the jury understands. This requires asking questions with the expert's mind and listening with the juror's ear.

The attorney and the expert witness should always remember that the audience is the jury. It is important that good information be provided, but it is equally important that it be provided in a way the jurors understand. If the jurors do not understand what is said, then it is as if the information was never presented.

By engaging in an easy, fluid conversation with the witness, the attorney can guide the jury through the technical material. Thus the lawyer should ask questions that naturally follow from the expert's responses. Ideally, the attorney will ask the exact follow-up questions that the jurors would ask if they could. The attorney must show genuine interest in the witness's answers, and the expert's answer to one question should naturally spark the next question.

Good court testimony has a natural flow to it, but such flow is nearly impossible if the attorney attempts to adhere strictly to a list of planned questions. When the lawyer, in the guise of preparation, has scripted all of the questions he or she wants to ask, and then asks them regardless of what the expert says or how the jury reacts, spontaneity is lost. It is spontaneity that helps keep the jurors' interest.

When an attorney uses an extensive script of planned questions, he or she is apt to ask a question and then busy him- or herself reviewing the next scripted question. When there is silence again, after the witness has answered, the attorney asks the next question on the list. The lawyer who does this clearly fails to listen intently to the witness's answers. Instead of creating a natural conversation, this style leads to a rigid, often unproductive, exchange of words.

To ask good questions, the trial lawyer must be a good *listener*. The attorney must listen carefully to the witness's answers to be certain they are accurate and that they are the answers he or she anticipated to the questions asked, and to determine whether any additional follow-up questions are needed to elicit more complete information.

When the attorney is completely familiar with the material that is the subject of the expert's testimony, he or she is able to have a fluid conversation with the witness. This knowledge, plus active listening, can best ensure that the information given by the expert witness is clear and accurate.

Instead of writing out all the questions to be asked of the expert witness, it is better for the attorney to prepare a guide to the *topics* of the direct examination. Some specific key questions might be written out, but too much reliance on an extensive, detailed script can make for a stiff and ineffective presentation of evidence. Alternatively, the lawyer might elect to write out specific questions but rely on the list only as a framework or a crutch. The skilled attorney will always attempt to engage the witness in an active dialogue.

It is not enough for the witness merely to offer opinions or theories; the witness must tell the jury why he or she holds those opinions or subscribes to those theories. Through the questioning, the attorney should give the witness the opportunity to teach the jury about the principles involved that are the basis for the expert's opinions. Effective expert testimony teaches *why* in addition to *what*.

The attorney should take steps to enhance the likelihood that the jurors will understand the technical evidence being presented. Jurors will be more likely to understand scientific or technical evidence if it can be explained in terms with which they are already familiar. The attorney might elect to use *hypothetical questions* that provide an educational background before beginning to discuss the specifics of the case. Similarly, presenting expert testimony by utilizing *analogies* to topics the jurors understand can be very effective. In this regard jury selection can play a very important role in the presentation of expert witness testimony. During jury selection, the attorney can learn about the backgrounds of the individual jurors, and thus can determine to some extent the subjects jurors are likely to know about. The attorney should share that information with the expert witness before the witness testifies. The two of them can then work together to make the expert's testimony individualized to the specific jurors. Again, the attorney and the expert witness should always remember the audience they are trying to educate.

Part of the attorney's job, as I have noted repeatedly, is to become well versed in the expert's field of practice. This is important so that the attorney will be able to elicit the most and best information from the expert witness. However, if it is not used properly, too much information can be dangerous.

The attorney should use the knowledge he or she has gained to guide the expert, not to show off that information to the jury. The attorney may sometimes be tempted to prove just how smart he or she has become, but that temptation should be resisted. The attorney must remember why expert testimony is used: to teach. The judge and jury might be impressed with how smart the lawyer is, but that does not mean they have become smart because of it. The attorney's goal is to teach the jurors, not to impress them.

The other danger of the attorney's having too much knowledge is the temptation he or she then faces of talking to the witness in the professional's vocabulary. When that occurs, it means the attorney is failing to communicate in layperson's terms. Again, the attorney must remember who the audience is, and why. The jurors need to learn. For the lawyer and witness, that means talking in a way the jurors understand. When the lawyer uses too many technical terms, or cites research articles just to show how smart he or she is, it doesn't help the jurors learn. The lawyer's task is to take technical, novel information and present it in a simple and understandable manner. For the skilled trial lawyer, intelligence is a tool to be used, not a toy to be displayed.

❑ **Considerations for the Expert Witness Presenting Testimony in Court**

The effective expert witness is able to present new and specialized material to the jury in a way they can understand and are willing to accept. The effective expert witness will be perceived as credible and intelligent. The effective expert witness will be perceived as knowing a lot, although he or she explains that knowledge simply. The effective expert witness is articulate and comfortable.

What Not to Do

To present expert testimony most effectively, the attorney should remember the following:

Don't expect the expert witness to teach the jury alone. The witness is dependent upon your questions.

Don't rely too much on prepared questions. *Listen* to the witness's answers.

Don't forget that the goal is to get the jury to understand what the witness is talking about and to trust the opinions and work of the expert witness.

Don't try to show off to the jury (or judge) how much you know. Remember who the audience is.

Don't indulge in overkill. Keep it simple.

It is a sad commentary, but nonetheless true, that in court, perceived credibility is more important than actual credibility. Jurors will rely upon the opinions of those witnesses they think they can trust. They might decide to rely upon the charlatan rather than the master because they perceive that the charlatan is more credible. It is the job of the witness and the attorney not only to be smart and professional, but also to be perceived that way. Following are some of the points expert witnesses should remember so that they can best present themselves and their knowledge in the courtroom:

> *In court, perceived credibility is more important than actual credibility.*

- Looks count.
- Demeanor counts.
- Be prepared.
- Tell the truth.
- Be yourself.
- Speak English.
- Know your audience.
- Say it three times.
- Get three opinions into one.

- Use the literature.
- Be the witness; don't try to be the lawyer.

LOOKS COUNT

As a television advertisement for shampoo proclaimed, "You only make a first impression once." This is very true in court. The fact finder is going to make an immediate judgment about the witness based upon first appearances. The expert witness must, therefore, not only sound like an expert and behave like an expert; the witness must also look like an expert. This means dressing appropriately for court. It is inexcusable for an expert witness to appear in court in informal or unclean clothing. A courtroom is a place of special business, and it demands formality. Judges wear robes and sit in an elevated position; flags of country and state are displayed; people stand as a sign of respect. The expert witness must honor that formality by dressing as a professional. The courtroom is not the place to make a novel fashion statement or check out the reaction to a new nose ring.

In addition to being neatly groomed, expert witnesses should consider what allegiances they, literally, wear on their sleeves. Sometimes, for example, witnesses in child abuse cases are cross-examined on being more "advocates for children" than objective experts. If an expert expects that line of questioning, it might be appropriate for him to forgo wearing a "Save the Children" necktie—jurors might view that as more pandering than fashionable. A more subtle accessory, such as a lapel pin, might not raise that concern.

DEMEANOR COUNTS

Upon entering the courtroom, the expert witness should be respectful to the court and court staff. Besides being good manners, this is important in establishing the witness's perceived credibility. Jurors are likely to be in the presence of the court staff for several days. The bailiff or law clerk is often the jury's only source of outside contact, and jurors frequently develop a sense of affection for that person. Any action by the witness that could be construed as rude or discourteous to court staff could have disastrous effects.

Verbal appearance is as important as physical appearance. The expert witness comes into court with a certain aura of respectability, and he or she can sustain that by sounding like a professional. The expert should strive to behave in as calm and courteous a manner as possible. If the witness appears nervous, jurors might interpret that as confusion, uncertainty, or dishonesty.

While giving testimony, the witness should speak with confidence and clarity. It is difficult to ask jurors to have confidence in the opinions of an expert when the expert's confidence itself appears in doubt. The witness should also be polite to all attorneys present.

BE PREPARED

As I have discussed at length in Chapter 3, the expert witness must be prepared. It is indefensible for an expert witness to come to court without an intimate familiarity with the facts of the case. There is no quicker way for the witness to lose the respect of a jury than to respond to introductory questions by thumbing through a large and disorganized file, muttering, "Let's see, the dates are in here someplace" or "Did you say my client's name was *Sally* Smith?" In every way, the expert witness must always appear professional and organized.

The witness may bring his or her files to court, and, as noted in Chapter 3, may also bring a summary or outline of the file. However, the witness should be aware that any piece of paper he or she brings to the witness stand may be examined by the opposing side. Some kind of guide may be helpful, but it should be prepared with the expectation that the cross-examining attorney will have the opportunity to review it as well.

TELL THE TRUTH

The expert witness must tell the truth—always, in every case, in response to all questions.

That might be enough said on this topic, but, alas, this point cannot be overemphasized. There is no surer way for an expert witness to lose complete credibility with a judge or jury than to be caught in a lie. The most frustrating aspect of this potential problem is that most

Be Careful What You Bring
With You Into Court

A witness is entitled to bring files, notes, and other documents into court to consult while testifying. However, the opposing counsel has the right to review those documents if the witness looks at them. This occurs procedurally when the witness refers to a particular document. The attorney then asks: "Excuse me, Dr. X, you just looked at a certain piece of paper. May I take a look at what you are reading from, please?" The judge is virtually certain to grant that request even if the witness or the other attorney objects.

One particular witness took advantage of this opportunity to bring a summary of his file with him to court. The cross-examination of this witness was particularly hostile. It was clear that the witness and the defense attorney had done battle before and that there was no love lost between them. Near the end of the testimony, the witness referred to his summary to help locate a document in his file. The lawyer then quickly demanded to see the summary document.

On top of the summary, the witness had written: "Use if asked by TJC." The defense attorney's name was Crawford, but his initials were not TJ.* Thinking the notation may be important, the attorney asked, "What does TJC stand for?"

The expert, fearing embarrassment, tried to avoid the question until he was ordered by the judge to answer: "That jerk Crawford." Although the jurors generally shared that view at the time, the comment, jurors later said, sharply diminished the professionalism of the witness in their eyes.

---

*The initials and name have been altered to protect the attorney's true identity. Actually, the "J" has also been altered, from "A," to make this a bit more polite.

of the lies that usually catch up to expert witnesses are lies about relatively insignificant material, such as some of the details of the expert's qualifications. A "padded" résumé is the easiest thing for opposing attorneys to check (see the discussion in Chapter 7), and the most foolish way for the expert witness to lose credibility. A high school teenager might pad a résumé to try to get a job and suffer few repercussions, but the expert witness is not a high schooler. Review the exchange from *State v. Werlein* (1989) that is presented boxed in Chapter 2, and consider the impact that had on the witness's credibility. No matter how smart or helpful the expert witness might have been, that exchange forever cost him his credibility. When that is gone, not much else matters.

BE YOURSELF

It may be helpful for a first-time expert witness to go to a courtroom to listen to a colleague testify so as to gain an appreciation for what a courtroom looks like, how the process works, and how the colleague handles testifying. The witness, however, should be careful not to try to copy someone else's style. The expert witness should not try to be anything, or anyone, other than who he or she is.

The most effective presentation is, as suggested above, a nice, albeit formal, discussion between attorney and witness, with the jury looking on. This should have the feel of a natural conversation. Other than the formality of dress and language required in court, the witness should not behave differently from the way he or she would outside of court. The witness should not try to adopt a court persona that is different from who he or she really is.

Some steps can be taken to enhance the expert's comfort while testifying. For instance, an effort might be made to allow the witness to take the physical position that is most comfortable for him or her. As I have noted previously, many experts are teachers, and some may be more comfortable talking while standing rather than sitting. Witness and attorney should discuss how the expert is most comfortable during their pretrial conversations. If the expert indicates that he or she would be more comfortable testifying while standing instead of sitting, the attorney should attempt to accommodate that. The attorney, by way of illustration, may be able to move the witness to a blackboard to make a drawing or a chart, and then, while the witness is still standing by the board, may continue the direct examination, allowing the witness to testify while remaining on his or her feet.

The attorney and the witness should discuss pretrial where the witness should look when responding to questions. Making proper eye contact with jurors is important, but it is sometimes awkward. Some witnesses look at the attorney while questions are being asked and then swivel and face the jury when responding. For some that is comfortable; for others, it is feels very unnatural. The witness must do what makes him or her feel most at ease.

In certain jurisdictions, attorneys are required to stand at a podium when interrogating witnesses. In other jurisdictions, attorneys are allowed the freedom to ask questions from anywhere in the court-room. In the latter courtrooms in particular, the witness should look at the attorney when answering questions. This enables the attorney to position him- or herself where the attorney wants the witness to look. For example, if the attorney wants the witness to look at the jury, the attorney will stand by the jury box. When in doubt, the witness should do what he or she finds most comfortable, whether it is looking at the attorney or at the jury.

SPEAK ENGLISH

It makes no sense to perform a professional evaluation, be well versed in the literature, and have an opinion that will be especially enlightening to the jury and then have that information lost in court because the jargon used to articulate it is unintelligible or unclear. The expert witness must talk in a way that is understood by layper-sons.

Most expert witnesses have obtained advanced college degrees. They have passed multiple examinations testing their knowledge of their particular fields of study. They may have conducted research or written learned articles for publication. In all these circumstances, they have been required to learn and use a vocabulary of specialized words. When the witness enters the courtroom, however, all those fancy words are best left at the office. Technical language can leave the jury more bewildered than enlightened, more perplexed than persuaded. The expert witness must speak in a way that the jury understands, and that generally means at a high school level. It is *USA Today*-speak.

Using big words might seem impressive, but if the words are not understood, they serve no value. Often there are more understandable words that can be used in place of technical terms. If the jury does not understand what the witness says, it might as well not have been said. It is one thing, for example, to claim, "Pharmaceutical intervention demonstrated efficacy," however, it is far more helpful to say, "Using drugs helped." When Jeffrey Dahmer was tried for the murder and mutilation of 15 young males, many of the world's leading psychiatric and psychological experts testified. In the end, the jurors told news reporters that the expert testimony only confused them. "The professional words were confusing," one juror was quoted as telling the Associated Press.

Speaking in words that allow one to be understood is different from being simple. The expert must be careful not to be so simplistic in his or her vocabulary as to appear condescending to the jurors. Most experts, however, have experience in the need to use understandable language. Professionals are called upon on a daily basis to explain things to their patients and clients. The way a doctor explains a diagnosis to a young patient is much the same way an opinion can be explained to a jury. Telling a client about the process of treatment usually involves the use of easy-to-understand concepts. Difficult terms should be explained to a jury with a similar degree of simplicity.

When a witness uses a specialized term, he or she should be prepared to define it immediately in a simple way. A doctor testifying about surface injuries on an assault victim, for example, might use the terms *contusion* and *ecchymosis*—those are the professional words. The expert should then describe what those words mean in everyday language; for example, "Ecchymosis is the discoloration you see on the skin when it is bruised. It really is a big word for black-and-blue mark" and "A contusion is a bruise in which the skin is not broken."

Perhaps the best way to explain technical concepts to a jury is through the use of analogies. If the expert witness can explain terminology, theories, syndromes, and unusual behaviors by making comparisons to everyday occurrences, the points can be more easily understood. For example, in a physical assault case, "skin elasticity" can be explained in terms of a rubber band. An agarose gel, used in electrophoresis, can be described as "a Jell-o like substance."

An Analogy Everyone Can Understand

A medical doctor was testifying in a child sexual abuse case involving the digital penetration of the child's vagina. She was attempting to explain why the fact that the child's vaginal opening was smaller than the circumference of the defendant's finger was of no significance. The doctor talked at length of elasticity and flexibility of tissue, but the defense attorney persisted that the size disparity proved his client's innocence. Finally, the doctor turned to an analogy: "Let me explain it to you this way, Mr. [defense attorney]," she began. "I could not measure the opening of your anus and determine the size of the largest stool you ever passed." That the jury understood.

It is always best for the expert witness to communicate concepts in the language of the listener. The most effective analogies, therefore, are those drawn from subjects familiar to the jurors. Analogies can be used to describe many items and concepts that arise in cases of interpersonal violence. For example, a colposcope can be described for the jury as being like "a pair of binoculars mounted on a stick, with a really strong flashlight on it." A concept such as the amount of force needed to cause an injury can be described as "as if the child fell from a 10-story building" or "a force comparable to a head-on car collision at 50-60 miles per hour." Learned helplessness can be explained with the analogy, "It's like the pet dog whose master always beats him when he comes home; yet the dog, dutifully and hopefully, continues to greet his master at the door every night."

KNOW YOUR AUDIENCE

During the jury selection process, the lawyers have the opportunity to learn about the individual jurors. The occupations and personal interests of the jurors are usually discussed during that process.

This exchange allows the lawyers to discover what subjects jurors are likely to know most about.

The attorney should inform the expert witness before trial of the backgrounds of some of the jurors. This will enable the witness and lawyer to discuss how best to teach these 12 people. They may try to determine some appropriate analogies that will be helpful to explain the witness's testimony.

For example, in one case the attorney had a strong feeling that the jury would select as foreperson a woman juror who raised horses for a living, so the attorney and expert witness decided that the witness should explain certain psychological phenomena by employing analogies to animal behavior. Similarly, in a case in which complex scientific evidence was used, the expert witnesses were advised that several of the jurors worked for a local airplane manufacturing company. The experts were then able to devise analogies that related facets of their work to various processes in the manufacture of an airplane. In another case, in preparing for a pretrial hearing in which the judge needed to decide whether to admit certain psychological evidence, the attorney told the expert witness that the judge was a golf addict; the witness was then able to craft analogies to golf addictions to explain certain behavioral traits of the victim (the judge permitted the testimony).

SAY IT THREE TIMES

A principal component of education is repetition. People learn better when important points are repeated in slightly different ways. A high level of repetition is of particular value in presenting expert witness testimony. Repetition helps the jury to understand good clinical practice as well as to understand the evidence in the particular case.

Understanding Good Clinical Practice

The expert wants the jury to know that he or she has engaged in good clinical practice in reaching his or her opinions in the case, but jurors do not know what good clinical practice is. They must, then, be taught. The following questions and answers (using a scenario of a medical evaluation) demonstrate how the jury can be taught through repetition:

Question: Doctor, in medical school did you receive any training in how to conduct an examination of a child who was suspected of being a victim of sexual abuse?

Answer: Yes, I did.

Question: And what did they teach you?

Answer: To do "a," then "b," then "c," then "d."

Question: When you went into the practice where you now work, did your colleagues teach you how they did these medical examinations?

Answer: Yes, they did.

Question: What did they teach you?

Answer: To do "a," then "b," then "c," then "d."

Question: Have you gone to professional conferences where the leaders of the field have provided ongoing training on how to conduct medical examinations of children suspected of being sexually abused?

Answer: Yes, I have gone to several such conferences.

Question: What did the leading professionals in your field teach you about how to conduct a medical examination of a child suspected of being sexually abused?

Answer: To do "a," then "b," then "c," then "d."

Question: Is there professional literature and research that offers advice on how to conduct a state-of-the-art medical examination of a child suspected of being sexually abused?

Answer: Yes there is, and I stay very current in reading that research.

Question: What does the literature in your field teach about how to conduct a state-of-the-art medical examination of a child suspected of being sexually abused?

Answer: To do "a," then "b," then "c," then "d."

Question: Let me ask you, hypothetically, if a 7-year-old girl came into your office with a history of having been sexually abused, how would you go about performing a medical examination on her?

Answer: I would do "a," then "b," then "c," then "d."

Question: Doctor, on April 12 of this year, did you see 7-year-old Sally Victim?

Answer: Yes, I did. She came into my office with a history of being sexually abused and I performed a medical examination upon her.

Question: Doctor, how did you proceed to conduct that examination?

Answer: Well, I did "a," then "b," then "c," then "d."

This repetition of how to conduct an examination teaches the jury how a good doctor conducts a state-of-the-art examination on a child suspected of being the victim of sexual abuse. The jurors are told five times how a good doctor should do such an examination, and when, in the end, they learn how this doctor performed the examination, the jurors' likely reaction is to use their newfound wisdom and conclude: "Great, the doctor did it right!" Similar sequences of questioning are useful whether the expert did a medical examination, was involved in providing therapy, did a scientific test, or engaged in any other professional process.

Understanding the Evidence in the Particular Case

The attorney and expert witness should attempt to explain the significant findings in a case in as many ways as possible. Because the conclusions are a key part of the expert's testimony, it is vital that the jury hear them clearly and often. One method of repeating the conclusions is for the attorney to have the expert witness explain the findings using different forms of media. The witness will have the opportunity to offer his or her opinions verbally, and should also consider how his or her conclusions can be displayed graphically. Again, consider the case above involving the medical diagnosis of sexual abuse.

Assume that a doctor has found evidence of a penetrating injury she believes was caused by abuse. The doctor will first be able to explain her findings verbally. However, these conclusions might also be explained visually. The key is for attorney and witness to *take their time* and not rush through the presentation of the evidence in all its various formats.

First, the witness can verbally offer a description of what was found. The attorney may consider having the doctor then go to a chalkboard or writing tablet to draw an illustration of the injury and provide a second description working from that drawing. The witness can next describe her findings by showing a slide of a normal child (for excellent photographs, see Heger & Emans, 1992) and discuss what things should look like and how this case is different. The witness can then proceed to use the slides showing the injured child. In each method, the jurors are provided with progressively more information. As the witness and attorney go over the material several times, jurors also get to test themselves silently to see if they understand what the witness has previously said.

When there is less graphic evidence, the witness might be asked to explain his or her opinion verbally, then be invited to highlight certain points on a chart or table. The witness can also provide this repetitious information through the attorney's asking increasingly more detailed questions. For example, a therapist might be asked to explain his conclusions in a narrative format. The attorney should remain quiet until the witness has completed the *entirety* of his answer. Then, when the witness is done, the attorney should go back to the beginning and ask specific questions, cuing the expert to go through the process a second time, responding to more precise questions. When that is done, the attorney may go through it all a third time, triggering the witness to discuss specific events or issues that occurred, or using visual aids. Through this repetition, the jury might understand a concept the third time that eluded them the first and second times through. (By asking for slightly more detailed information each time, the attorney should avoid restrictions on testimony that is "cumulative.")

Too often, the expert witness and the attorney skip immediately to the final stage: They use slides and pictures when they tell the story the first time. This provides the jurors with only one opportunity to learn. It does not allow the jurors multiple opportunities to appreciate and comprehend fully the material presented to them. It also generally provides only conclusions, and not the reasons jurors should accept those conclusions.

The importance of expert testimony mandates that the jurors understand certain key issues. Time and care should be taken to go through the material in sufficient detail, and in various ways, to enhance the jury's opportunity to learn. The effective presentation of expert testimony requires that the witness and the attorney take their time to deliver the evidence in a repetitive and educational format.

GET THREE OPINIONS INTO ONE

The attorney may turn the expert's opinion into multiple opinions. An expert witness is entitled to rely upon otherwise inadmissible evidence in forming his or her opinions. The opinions of other experts with whom an expert consulted are traditionally inadmissible hearsay evidence. However, if the witness has "reasonably relied upon" those opinions in coming to his or her conclusions, the witness is likely entitled to share that in court (Federal Rules of Evidence 703).[1]

When the witness has consulted with other experts, that point should be brought out before the jury. In this way, one opinion can be turned into multiple opinions. The following exchange offers an example:

Question: Dr. Smith, you told us earlier that in reaching your opinion you reviewed the literature in this field.

Answer: That is correct, I reviewed the leading articles on this issue.

Question: Doctor, who is John Green?

Answer: Dr. Green is the world's leading authority on the subject we have been discussing. He has written about a dozen books on the subject and is well regarded for his opinions on this topic.

Question: Before reaching your final opinion, did you take the time to contact Dr. Green?

Answer: In fact I did. I wanted to consult with him about this case. We had three telephone conversations about this case.

Question: Did you share with him the information you had at hand?

Answer: Yes, I sent him some of the materials and summarized others. In our discussions, he asked me certain questions that I was able to answer, and we only concluded our talks when he indicated he had all the information he needed.

Question: Did Dr. Green offer you his opinion about the facts of this case?

Answer: He did. Dr. Green said he agreed with my conclusions in this case.

Question: Is the opinion of Dr. Green about this topic a piece of information that experts in this field would reasonably rely upon in forming their own opinions about this subject?

Answer: Absolutely. Dr. Green's opinion would be greatly relied upon by experts in this field.

Question: Specifically, what was Dr. Green's opinion?[2]

This type of testimony can be presented in cases where experts consult with their coworkers, colleagues in the area, virtually anyone whose opinions would ordinarily be relied upon in forming an opinion. This rule provides an excellent mechanism for introducing multiple opinions through one expert.[3]

USE THE LITERATURE

It is important for the expert witness to be knowledgeable about the state of the literature in his or her field of practice. During the course of the witness's testimony it may be appropriate to discuss a particularly significant article.

The witness should be careful not to get bogged down in the details of research, because that will cause the jury to lose interest. It is vital that the witness remember that the audience is a lay jury: The witness is not presenting to a group of professional colleagues. The point is to teach, not to show off intelligence.

Certain articles, however, can prove particularly helpful to illustrate specific points. For example, in the following testimony a medical expert explains why certain bruises to a child could not have been caused by an accidental fall from a bed, as the defense alleges. This excerpt picks up after the expert has testified that the injuries did not appear to have been caused by a fall from a bed.

Question: You indicated that the journal *Pediatrics* is an important reference for you in your field.

Answer: That's correct.

Question: Are you familiar with an article published in October of 1977 dealing with injuries resulting when small children fall out of bed?

Answer: Yes, I am.

Question: Have you had a chance to review that article?

Answer: I have.

Question: Was the information contained in that article helpful to you at all in trying to determine whether there is a likelihood that the injuries [the child victim] sustained could have been caused by falling out of a bed some four to four and a half feet?

Answer: Yes.

Question: Why is that?

Answer: Well, in that article researchers found that . . . .

The expert is then able to explain the research in the article, what the findings were, and why they hold particular significance for the instant case. The article is used as a reference. It is used to teach the jury and to show information that the witness relied upon. Kept simple, that information can be very helpful to the fact finders.

BE THE WITNESS; DON'T TRY TO BE THE LAWYER

The witness's job is to answer questions. The lawyer's job is to ask questions and to object to the opposing lawyer's questions. The lawyer cannot be the witness, and the expert witness should not try to be the lawyer.

The expert witness should not volunteer information when giving testimony. If the attorney has not asked for certain information, the expert witness should not attempt to provide it. The expert witness should not answer questions that he or she thinks should have been asked, but were not. There may be valid legal reasons the lawyer has not asked specific questions. The witness's volunteering information beyond what the questions call for may jeopardize the case. For example, a certain answer may violate a prior court order limiting testimony, and the expert's unsolicited response may result in a mistrial. Alternatively, the volunteered response may run counter to tactical decisions made by the attorney. The expert witness should accept that—he or she should just answer the questions asked, and not try to help.

Further, the expert witness should not try to make evidentiary rulings while being a witness. "I can't answer that, it calls for hearsay," are words that should never come out of an expert witness's mouth. There are 73 rules in the Federal Rules of Evidence, most of which have required the interpretation of appellate court judges. When an attorney asks a question, the witness should not attempt to decide if it violates one of those 73 rules (e.g., is hearsay)—that is the attorney's job. A question may indeed be improper, or may fall within some exception to an evidence rule, or may be objectionable, but for tactical reasons the opposing attorney may elect not to object. The witness must let the lawyers decide such issues. The expert has enough to do just being a witness.

❏ **Degree of Certainty**

There is no need for the expert witness to try to oversell his or her opinion. If the witness cannot be definitive, he or she should say so. If the witness's opinion is not conclusive but merely eliminates certain other possibilities, he or she should make that clear. There is no reason for the expert to overreach.

The law does not require that expert witnesses be absolutely certain of their opinions before giving them: "Diagnosis need not be based upon certainty, but may be based upon probability; the lack of absolute scientific certainty does not deprive the opinion of evidentiary value" (*People v. Mendible*, 1988, p. 562).

The lack of absoluteness in the opinions of the expert witness goes to the weight of the evidence only. "Expert testimony couched in terms of 'could have,' 'possible,' or 'similar' is uniformly admitted at trial. The lack of certainty goes to the weight to be given the testimony, not to its admissibility. This is so, in part, because the scientific process involved often allows no more certain testimony" (*State v. Lord*, 1991). As legal commentators Louisell and Mueller (1992) have observed: "The fact that an expert cannot be categorical, and admits of some uncertainty in his conclusions, does not mean that his testimony should be excluded or that it fails the helpfulness requirement. . . . [An expert's] inability to be definitive should not stand in the way of receiving his testimony" (§ 382).

These legal rules should help to make the expert comfortable in presenting courtroom testimony. There is no need for the expert witness to say more than he or she believes. These principles reinforce all of the other concepts of good testimony for the expert witness: Be honest, be professional, be comfortable, and remember that the job of the expert witness is merely to provide quality education to the jury.

❏ Notes

1. The opinions must be "of a type reasonably relied upon by experts in the particular field in forming opinions or inferences upon the subject" (Federal Rules of Evidence 703).

2. This question might be objected to. It is a permissible question under ER 703 if the proper foundation is made. If the objection is sustained, the same information can be obtained by asking, "If Dr. Green had an opinion different from yours, would that have caused you to reevaluate your conclusion?" When this is answered in the affirmative, the follow-up question is asked, "Did you reevaluate your conclusion?" This would then be answered in the negative.

3. Of course, this course of action is not without risk. In talking with other experts, the attorney and the expert may obtain an adverse opinion. In that case, the attorney is likely ethically bound to reveal that counter opinion to the opposing side. See note 4 in Chapter 3.

5

Dealing With Cross-Examination

> *It is hard for a cross-examiner to win his case on cross-examination; it is easy for him to lose it.*
>
> McCormick's Handbook
> on the Law of Evidence, 1972

And now it is the other side's turn.

The expert witness is generally retained by one side, prepared by one side, and, in many regards, is aligned with one side. Cross-examination is the time when the adverse party seeks to attack what the expert witness has said. It is often viewed as a frightening time for the expert witness.

If the expert witness is well prepared, however, cross-examination need not be a time for concern. This chapter discusses how the expert witness can effectively deal with cross-examination. If the expert witness is prepared and focused, cross-examination can be nothing more than a second opportunity for the witness to offer and clarify his or her opinions and conclusions for the jury.

In preparing for and encountering cross-examination, the expert witness should keep seven basic points in mind:

1. Remember that the opposing attorney is likely every bit as nervous as you.
2. As an expert witness, you have considerable control over how the cross-examination is conducted.
3. Listen, listen, listen to the question.
4. Understand that cross-examination is not a professional debate or a search for truth; rather, it is an assault made as part of an adversarial process.
5. Always consider how you would deal with the questions asked if they were asked in the real world.
6. Always be professional.
7. Always be honest.

In the pages that follow, I offer specific tips and suggestions for how expert witnesses can respond to certain situations based on the seven points set forth above. Many of these concepts are equally applicable to the giving of effective *direct* testimony, as discussed in Chapter 4.

The expert witness should also review Chapter 7, where I give suggestions to attorneys on how to cross-examine the irresponsible expert witness effectively. The responsible witness would be well-advised to review those suggestions to gain additional understanding of how the opposing attorney might proceed. All witnesses should seek to avoid the pitfalls of the irresponsible expert witness.

❏ The Opposing Attorney Is Likely Nervous Too

Consider the pressure on the opposing attorney. A bright, articulate professional has just come into court and provided education and guidance to the jury. The witness has offered his or her opinions about a certain set of facts in an understandable and credible fashion.

The opinions offered have severely hurt the opposing side's chances of victory. Now that side's lawyer must stand up and make the damage go away.

The lawyer must convince the jury that the expert witness's opinions are wrong, irrelevant, and/or not worthy of belief. Not only is the attorney going to attempt to accomplish one or all of these tasks, but everyone in the courtroom (including the jurors) is expecting him or her to do so with great panache. Every juror has seen how expert witnesses are reduced to rubble in television dramas and movies; they expect nothing less here. And if that were not enough, the lawyer must do all this generally in one of two ways: by discrediting the testimony or by discrediting the witness.

Thus cross-examination requires the attorney either to debate the professional in the professional's field of expertise or to assail the witness's credibility, but to do so without being so disrespectful that the jury becomes sympathetic to the witness. This is not easy, and, not surprisingly, very few trial attorneys are particularly good at it. Most experienced trial lawyers would agree that cross-examining a good expert witness is the most difficult thing a lawyer must do in a trial. Although the expert witness may be apprehensive about the impending cross-examination, he or she can be assured that the attorney is probably every bit as uneasy.

Frequently, when a cross-examiner becomes frustrated, his or her questions will become more hostile, even obnoxious. It might be hard for the witness to appreciate this at the time, but when the tone of cross-examination increases in its combativeness, it generally means that the attorney realizes he or she is losing this battle. If the witness can remember that, he or she can draw strength from it. The lesson is this: The nastier the questions become, generally, the better the cross-examination is going for the witness.[1]

A good cross-examiner can smell blood and knows how to exploit a weakness, but a good witness can likewise smell victory. The nastier the attorney gets, the calmer the expert witness should become. The more frantic the lawyer acts during cross-examination, the more relaxed the witness should act. The visual and audible distinctions between them will help tell the jury just who is winning this professional war.

❏ The Witness Has Considerable Control

For the trial attorney, the key to a successful cross-examination is to be in complete control of the witness. A skilled cross-examiner attempts to obtain and exercise that control. It is not surprising, therefore, that many witnesses express frustration at what they perceive to be their complete lack of control during the course of giving testimony. In truth, however, the skilled expert witness maintains considerable control over what occurs in the courtroom battle with the cross-examining attorney. The witness merely needs to recognize how to exercise that control.

The witness can test his or her control by making simple requests, such as asking for a bathroom break or a glass of water. In either situation, the court is certain to accommodate the witness's request. Similarly, the witness can exercise control over more frustrating aspects of the courtroom experience. If an attorney is talking too fast, engaging in intimidation techniques, asking complicated or misleading questions, or cutting off the witness's answers, the witness can remedy those situations. The witness must only recognize that he or she has that ability.

First, the witness must avoid obvious mistakes:

- A witness should never answer a question he or she does not understand.
- A witness should never say that he or she agrees with a statement that he or she does not agree with.
- A witness should never allow him- or herself to become confused or distracted because an attorney is talking too fast or standing too close.

Witnesses do these things all the time, although they definitely should not.

If an attorney asks a question that the witness does not understand, the witness has the ability (and obligation) to ask that the question be rephrased. For example, a witness might say: "Excuse me, Mr. Matlock, would you please repeat the question? I'm afraid I didn't understand the question the way you asked it"; or "Please rephrase the question—it did not make sense to me the way you asked it."

If an attorney asks a question that is really several questions rolled into one, the witness should ask for clarification. Following are examples of how a witness might respond when this occurs:

- You are asking me three questions, Ms. Mason. I would say yes, I believe "x"; no, I do not think "y"; and no, "z" did not occur in this case.
- Well, you have asked four questions there, Mr. Bailey. My answers are yes, no, yes, yes.
- You have asked several questions, Ms. Clark. Which do you want me to answer first?
- Would you please rephrase the question? I think you are really asking several questions there.

Sometimes an attorney will try to disorient or fluster a witness by standing very close to him or her and/or talking loudly. The witness may properly, if politely, request that the lawyer move away and speak more quietly. For example:

- I'm sorry, Mr. Marshall, you were talking so loud I wasn't focusing. Do you think you could ask your question again without yelling it at me?
- Sir, I can hear you just fine, would you mind speaking a little softer? It's rather distracting when you talk that loud.

As for standing too closely:

- Ms. Kincaid, could you move back a little? It's uncomfortable having you stand this close. It makes it hard for me to concentrate on your questions, and I would like to be able to answer you as accurately as possible.

The expert witness should recognize that generally the attorney is purposely standing too close, talking too loud, and/or asking compound questions as a tactic. By politely asking the lawyer to stop, the witness is likely to expose that tactic. If the attorney persists, this polite reaction from the witness, repeated as necessary, will probably get the judge to intervene and certainly will win the jurors' sympathies. Either one is a victory.

Another trick that attorneys use is to progressively talk faster, trying to get the witness to talk faster, purposely moving to a frenetic pace, thinking that the faster the witness talks, the less he or she can concentrate on the questions. The expert witness should be able to recognize when this is occurring and should take this as the perfect time to ask for a glass of water, or to ask for a moment to ponder a specific answer.

Expert witnesses often mistakenly believe they appear smarter the more quickly they answer.

Expert witnesses often mistakenly believe they appear smarter the more quickly they answer. Consider the alternative—in response to a specific question by the defense attorney, the witness pauses and then responds:

> That's an interesting question; I'd like to think about that a moment. [Pause. Pause. Ponderous look upon the brow. Perhaps a scribble on a pad of paper. Pause. Reflection. Pause. Pause.] Okay, thank you. My answer is . . .

The jurors are likely to be more impressed by an answer that has obviously been carefully considered than one that is fired back at the same pace as the rapidly thrown question.

An attorney conducting cross-examination may try to misstate the witness's testimony, either by deleting something or by adding something. The expert witness should not allow that to happen. If a question is asked that misstates the witness's prior testimony, it should immediately be corrected:

Question: Doctor, you told us x, y, and z. Does that mean . . . ?
Answer: Actually, I didn't say x, y, and z. I said x and y [or I said x, y, z *and* a, b, and c].

In all of the situations mentioned above, the witness has the ability to force the lawyer to reword questions, to slow down, or to move away. If the attorney is doing something that makes it difficult for the witness to concentrate on the questions, the witness should say so. When the witness speaks up, it is likely to have an impact on the questioner as well as on the judge and jury.

❏ Questions Need Not Be Answered Yes or No

During cross-examination, the opposing attorney seeks to take control from the witness. The attorney's goal is to get the witness to respond quickly and without explanation. Lawyers are taught that every question on cross-examination should be framed so that the witness can merely agree. That is why most questions end with " . . . isn't that true, doctor?" or " . . . correct, ma'am?"

Many who teach cross-examination skills argue that the perfect cross-examination is nothing more than a long speech by the attorney with intermittent words of agreement by the witness. The witness's responses are not so much answers as they are punctuation. The effective expert witness recognizes this attempt by the attorney and does not allow him or her to succeed.

There is no requirement that a witness's answers be limited to yes or no responses.[2] If pressed by a cross-examiner for a yes/no response, the witness might consider some of these replies:

- I'm sorry, I cannot answer that yes or no. It's not that simple/ straightforward/black or white.
- Well, I can't answer that question yes or no without misleading the jury. [Now the attorney has two options: Rephrase the question or say, "That's okay, mislead the jury."]
- I'm sorry, I need you to rephrase the question; I cannot honestly answer that yes or no.

It is important for the witness to respond in full statements, not merely with agreement or disagreement with the questions. It should be the witness who provides education to the fact finder. By simply agreeing or disagreeing with the lawyer's questions, the expert witness permits the attorney to do the educating, and the expert's answers become no more than the time the attorney pauses for breath between questions. It must be the other way around: The expert witness must be the credible teacher. With a small bit of polite assertiveness, the witness can exercise considerable control over this process.

It is important for the witness to respond in full statements.

WHEN THE WITNESS'S ANSWER IS CUT OFF

A favorite tactic of the cross-examining attorney is to interrupt a response as soon as the attorney hears "the good part." An effective expert witness does not permit that to occur. When a lawyer cuts off an answer, the witness should be quick to seek to finish the response: "Excuse me, counsel, I wasn't finished with my answer"; or "Sorry, Mr. Harmon, don't you want me to complete my response?" Usually, the judge will permit the witness to continue his or her answer. In any event, the witness has signaled to the presenting attorney that this is an area that needs to be clarified in redirect.

If confronted by an attorney who is able to cut off answers repeatedly and a judge who is unwilling to allow the completion of those answers, the witness might remark to the judge: "Judge, I took an oath to tell the *whole* truth. I am not being allowed to do that. May I please provide the whole answer?"

STRESS MANAGEMENT TECHNIQUES

Even for the most experienced witness, testifying in court remains a stressful event. But all professionals have had experience with stressful events—every professional has encountered pressure situations, be they board examinations or professional presentations. Additionally, most adults have engaged in nonprofessional stressful activities: sporting competitions, public speaking, theatrical or musical performances. The same kinds of stress management techniques that are useful in those situations can be useful for the expert witness when he or she is called to court.

Effective stress management techniques that might be employed in the courtroom include muscle contraction/relaxation, deep breathing exercises, and creative visualization. One frequent expert witness, for example, upon taking the witness stand, visualizes her two large dogs sitting at her feet. "They'll keep the opposing attorney from hurting me," she thinks. If she feels particularly assailed in court, she looks down and "sees" her protective dogs, which instantly calms her.

Sometimes the witness is fearful in anticipation of a particular question or line of questioning that might be forthcoming. In that situation the witness must be certain to disclose the area of concern to the presenting attorney during pretrial preparation.

If an expert has been effectively cross-examined in a certain area in previous cases, that should also be brought to the attention of the presenting attorney. Instead of silently wishing that the cross-examination will not touch on those issues, the witness and the presenting attorney can probably devise a method for the witness to use in sidestepping or confronting those issues.

Some child abuse professionals have been questioned during cross-examination about whether they were themselves victims of abuse or whether they are gay.[3] Such inquiries, which are completely inappropriate, are generally used solely to intimidate the witness. If the expert witness has been asked such questions previously, he or she should alert the presenting attorney to that fact pretrial. By motions *in limine* the attorney can seek to prevent such questions from being asked.[4] Of course, the attorney can make such motions only if he or she is made aware, in advance, that such questions might be asked.

❏   **Listen, Listen, Listen to the Question**

The expert witness must listen carefully to each question asked and answer *only* the question asked. The expert witness should not answer the question he or she thinks the attorney *meant* to ask. Nor should the expert witness, ordinarily, volunteer more information than is necessary to answer the specific question.

The expert witness should listen intently to the question to be certain he or she fully understands the question before answering it. The expert witness should not answer a question he or she has heard only *part* of. The expert witness should not answer a question he or she understood only *most* of. The expert witness should answer only the precise question that is asked and understood.

If the question is at all unclear, the witness should ask to have it repeated or clarified. If the witness does not hear the question completely, he or she should ask to have it repeated in its entirety. If the expert witness thinks that a question that has been asked was really meant to inquire about something else, he or she should still answer only the question *as asked*.

The effective expert witness must be an intense listener. The witness invites complete disaster when he or she fails to answer the questions asked.

❏ **Cross-Examination Is Not a Professional Debate or a Search for Truth**

More often than not, the opposing attorney is concerned less with truth than with advocating effectively for his or her client. In the American judicial system, there is a distinction between what is true and what is fair. *Fair* refers to a case well tried by both parties with an opportunity to present evidence and arguments. It is hoped that from such fairness the truth will emerge—but this is not always the case. Judges are obligated to ensure procedural fairness of the trial process. That might not always result in the production of "the truth."

Cross-examination is an adversarial process. The cross-examining attorney tries to diminish the witness's opinion and/or credibility in the eyes of the jurors. Cross-examination is not a professional or intellectual debate.

Although the expert witness should be willing to consider additional information, he or she must also focus on the fact that while he or she is on the stand, it is his or her opinions that are being attacked. The witness should be prepared to defend his or her opinions and conclusions.

The expert witness should be careful not to become engaged in an intellectual discussion of issues that drifts away from the issues involved in the litigation. When the opposing attorney is well prepared, there might be a cross-examination that presents interesting or provocative professional issues. The witness might find him- or herself enjoying the collegial dialogue. However, more often than not, while the witness is taking delight in this challenging intellectual exchange, the attorney is sawing the witness's legs off. The witness would be wise to guard against that situation. If the witness is enjoying the cross-examination *too* much, something might be awry.

The expert witness similarly needs to guard against misleading questions. The cross-examiner might ask questions that on their face appear logical, but, when tied to the facts of the particular case, are foolish. For example, in a case in which a child suffered burn injuries from being dunked into very hot water, the medical expert testified about the significance of the burn pattern on the child's lower leg. The defense attorney tried to suggest in cross-examination that if the doctor's theory was correct, there would be greater burning at the top of the burn pattern: "Well doctor, heat rises, doesn't it? Yes or no." On its face, the answer is yes. But to suggest that heat rising would make the water hotter on top, thus altering the burn pattern, is ridiculous under the facts of the case. To simply respond yes or no is to answer a meaningless question. A better reply might be, "That theory is true, but it has no bearing on the facts of this case, because . . . ."

Another example is when the cross-examining attorney asks a question that cites literature slightly out of context: "Is there support in the literature for the notion that children frequently recant original allegations of being sexually abused?" The attorney is looking for one-word agreement. Technically, the answer is, "Yes, there is support for that notion." That answer alone, however, may be misleading. The defense attorney will use that concise answer to imply that, according to the expert, children's allegations of sexual abuse are unreliable because they are frequently recanted. The attorney will urge the jury to acquit, given that a recantation is likely to follow, according to the expert's testimony.

The expert witness should avoid the trap of providing a brief answer that is factually accurate but also misleading in the form it is given. That is best accomplished by providing a longer, more complete response. The response to the question above, then, might be as follows:

> There have been several well-respected articles published that deal with this subject. These articles document that children sometimes recant original allegations of sexual abuse. Such recantation often does not alter the truth of the original allegations. This view is widely accepted in the professional community. The literature explains that recantation can be a form of accommodation that occurs for several reasons. . . .

Thorough responses are necessary whenever misleading questions are asked. The witness should endeavor to prevent the attorney from allowing information to be provided to the jury that is inaccurate or out of context. When a short answer to a question would be misleading, the witness may properly indicate that. For example: "That is an interesting point, but it has nothing to do with this case"; or "Yes, that is possible, but that is not what happened here"; or "That is partially accurate, but to isolate that one factor is misleading. You must also give equal consideration to . . . ."

Another frequent trick used in cross-examination is for the attorney to incorporate the witness's last answer into the next question, but altered slightly:

Question: So, you would agree that the behavior of the mother may have influenced the child's disclosures?

Proper response: I said that was one of *several* factors to evaluate: You must consider the spontaneity of the disclosure, the context in which it was given, the vocabulary used, plus the other factors I have earlier mentioned, including the mother's behavior. No one factor can be looked at in isolation.

The examples above illustrate the benefit of the witness's answering all questions using short, positive statements. Whenever possible, the expert witness should avoid one- or two-word answers to questions on cross-examination. Instead, the witness should endeavor to make every response a brief and affirmative statement. In addition to keeping the information in perspective, this also affords the expert witness the opportunity to continue to restate his or her direct testimony.

❑ How Would the Witness Handle the Question in the Real World?

Why would a professional answer a question asked in his or her office in one fashion and then, if asked the very same question in court, answer it in a completely different fashion? There is no reason:

The expert witness should answer the question in the same way in both places.

When the cross-examiner asks detailed questions or refers to specific literature, the expert witness should respond in the same manner as if he or she were speaking with a colleague in the witness's office. In other words, the witness should consider how he or she would answer the question in the real world, and then try to answer it that way in court.

If, in the real world, a professional is asked his or her opinion about a certain research article, the professional is likely to elect to review the article first before responding. Why, then, would the witness answer the question any other way in the courtroom?

If, in the real world, a professional is asked about another expert's views, the professional might want to consult with that individual before declaring him or her to be right or wrong. Why, then, would the witness want to answer in any other way in the courtroom?

If the cross-examining attorney asks the expert witness about a particular article, the witness should do what he or she would likely do in the real world: ask to see the article. If the attorney does not produce a copy of the article, that of itself will likely prevent further discussion of the article in most jurisdictions. If the article is produced, the witness should *read it!*

In reviewing a specific article referred to by the cross-examining attorney, the witness should consider several issues:

- Does the article discuss an issue that is applicable to the case in court? Is the issue in the correct context? For example, is the debate in court about forensic evaluation of a client and the article about a therapeutic assessment? Does the article deal with adult survivors of sexual abuse and the trial involve allegations made by a child? Is the sample/database used in the article a fair comparison group considering the facts involved in the litigation?

- What is the date of the article? Does it reflect *current* state-of-the-art thinking on this topic? Much of the knowledge in issues related to child abuse litigation has evolved substantially in the past several years.

- Is the article published in a peer review journal?

- Is the author well respected in the field? Is this the lone voice in the field taking this position?

Dealing With Literature in Court
as in Real Life

The medical doctor had testified that the young male she had examined suffered from injuries that were, in her opinion, caused by sexual abuse. The defense attorney had tried to suggest that the injuries could, instead, have been caused by Crohn's disease. During cross-examination, the defense attorney produced an article on Crohn's disease and showed it to the doctor. Her responses were a textbook example of how to deal with this situation. All the time, she later said, she kept in her mind the advice: How would I deal with this question in the real world?

"Doctor, are you familiar with a Dr. J. M.?" the attorney began.

"Oh yes," she replied, "he is very well respected in my field."

"And are you familiar with a journal called . . . ," he continued, identifying the journal.

"Oh yes," the doctor replied, "it is a very well-respected, peer-reviewed journal."

And yes, she acknowledged she knew of a specific article published in that journal by Dr. M. that discussed Crohn's disease, and yes, that article is very well respected in the medical field.

"Well doctor, doesn't Dr. M. in this article identify the same injuries you saw and conclude they are more likely caused by Crohn's disease than by sexual abuse?"

The witness thought: What would I do if asked that question in the real world? First, she thought, she'd want to read the article again. "Do you have the article, counsel?" she asked.

He produced a copy and the doctor reviewed it, but the photographs, which were of key importance, were only black-and-white copies of the original color photographs. In the real world she knew that she would want to see the color pictures. "I would need to see the color photographs," she said, "to make any accurate comment."

The attorney produced a color reprint of the article.

(Continued)

"Well, give me some time to study these photographs again," she said, as much stalling for time as to examine them carefully. What would I do in the real world? she again thought.

"Counsel, you raise an interesting point. But I don't believe that Dr. M. would disagree with my conclusion. In this situation I would try to speak with him about this case and seek his opinion."

At this point the prosecutor interrupted: "Excuse me, Judge, the witness has indicated she would like to consult with Dr. M. I have Dr. M's phone number in my office. Could we take a 15-minute recess and give her that opportunity?"

A recess was taken, a phone call was made, and the two doctors consulted. The witness returned to the courtroom finally to answer the defense attorney's question.

"I have had the opportunity to consult with Dr. M. about this case, and he completely agrees with me that what we have in this situation is not Crohn's disease, but evidence of sexual abuse. Let me explain why . . . ."

- Is this the most recent writing by this author? Have the views of this author changed or been contradicted?
- Has this article been accepted or criticized in the field?

Expert witnesses who have been confronted by attorneys who have inappropriately used specific articles in cross-examination have provided these responses:

- Oh, I see you have the 1986 article by Dr. X. You should get the 1989 article he wrote, where he changes his opinion and adopts the same view I have expressed in court here.
- Yes, this article is very familiar to me. It is probably one of the most criticized articles in this field and represents a minority, and perhaps lone, view on this topic.
- The article you have referred to, counsel, talks about how *adults* respond in these circumstances. As I have mentioned, the research is well documented that children, such as Sally, react very differently in these situations.

❏   **Always Be Professional**

Being professional includes being courteous. It is not impressive when the expert witness is polite to the presenting attorney on direct examination and then turns belligerent when the cross-examining attorney says, "Good afternoon, doctor."

The expert witness should respond to questions on cross-examination in the same tone as in direct. Unless the cross-examining attorney's conduct becomes completely inappropriate, the witness is well-advised not to argue with the attorney. The better the witness is able to maintain his or her cool under pressure, the more professional, and thus convincing, he or she appears.

KNOW YOUR LIMITS

Being a professional also means the expert witness must recognize the limitations of his or her expertise. When the expert witness begins to wander beyond his or her true field of expertise, disaster lurks.

At first, most witnesses are a bit reluctant to be termed "experts." Once they get over that and start being asked their opinions about things, however, it can become very intoxicating. The witness must know where his or her true expertise stops. The failure of the witness to set reasonable boundaries will allow the skilled cross-examiner to have the witness recommending stocks and making Super Bowl predictions from the witness stand. Imposed humility is the price paid by the witness who gets greedy about expanding his or her expert opinions.

BE YOURSELF

All expert witnesses testify in court in slightly different ways. Some disdain appearing in court; others welcome the combative nature of the exchange. Those who appear with some frequency have developed skills to help them cope and prosper.

A witness who has not testified before might want to watch a colleague testify to get "a feel for the road." A professional might elect to hear the testimony of a well-known authority who has come into town to testify in a high-profile case. Listening to another

BOTTOM LINERS

©1995 Tribune Media Services, Inc.
All Rights Reserved.

5/9

"I'm impressed by your resume, Ferguson.
What am I overlooking?"

Reprinted by permission: Tribune Media Services.

testify might provide some support for the belief that giving testimony in court is a survivable process. However, one witness should never try to copy the style of another. Expert witnesses should be themselves when they testify. No witness can properly function in court when he or she is trying to be someone, or something, different from who he or she is. If the witness listens to the question, thinks about the answer before responding, and tells the truth, all will turn out right.

Humor is often used as a stress reduction technique. In court, humor does have its place, but it is very difficult to be both humorous and professional. The jury is going to make an assessment of the credibility of the witness and his or her information, usually in the early part of the witness's testimony. Humor, if used, should never be a part of the beginning of the testimony. Any joking the witness does should be spontaneous and directed toward a situation in court, not any individual. For example, if the witness is using a piece of audiovisual equipment that malfunctions, it might be acceptable to comment, "Now you see why I went to graduate/medical school." It is inappropriate for the witness to direct joking toward an individual. For example, if the cross-examining attorney is asking about a particular psychological test, the witness should not remark, "It would be quite interesting to see how *you* would score on the psychopathic deviate scale, Mr. Gordon."

❏ **Always Be Honest**

After all that has been said, one rule applies above all else in the courtroom: The expert witness must tell the truth—always, about everything.

That should be all that needs to be said about this topic, but, as I explore in more detail in Chapter 7, expert witnesses sometimes have a hard time with this.

THE EXPERT WITNESS AS ADVOCATE

In some instances the opposing attorney may try to suggest that the witness's version of truth is colored by other motives. One frequent area of cross-examination in cases of interpersonal violence involves attacking the objectivity of the witness as being an *advocate* for a particular position. A psychologist, for example, may treat only victims of crime, not offenders. A doctor who treats children may not have the opportunity to work on behalf of defendants. Either of these witnesses might be subject to cross-examination as being a biased, prosecution-oriented witness. By being honest, a witness can properly reject such a critique. The witness should be prepared to put this issue in perspective, which can be done in several ways:

- The witness can explain how he or she gets case referrals.

- The witness can explain that there may be professional or ethical constraints that bar him or her from treating different groups of individuals. (This could also include issues of licensure or certification. Alternatively, it could involve issues of local practice. In some jurisdictions, for example, local practice is that therapists do not treat both victims and offenders of sexual abuse.)

- The witness can discuss opportunities to offer differing viewpoints: "I offer my opinions to anyone who asks, counsel. I'd be happy to consult with you on these cases if you ask."

- The witness can admit what is obvious: "Of course I advocate for children. What responsible adult doesn't speak up on behalf of children?"

- The witness can distinguish between professional responsibilities and personal viewpoints.

- The witness can question the alternative: "Counsel, are you suggesting that I should be advocating that sexual abuse of children is a good thing?"

The best way for the witness to avoid becoming a biased advocate is by being professional. The expert's diagnosis or opinion should not be different depending upon who is asking the questions. The witness should not tailor his or her responses to fit a desired result.

A professional should be willing to review cases submitted by what is typically the opposing side. For example, a child psychologist who frequently testifies on behalf of the prosecution in child abuse cases about disclosure patterns of abused children should be willing to provide the same testimony if the defense asks. A medical doctor should be willing to review colposcopic slides submitted by the defense and offer an opinion about them.

If the same set of facts provides one answer to one party, but a different answer to an opposing party, then the professionalism and honesty of the witness *are* fairly subject to criticism.

HOW MUCH ARE YOU BEING PAID
FOR YOUR OPINION?

If the witness is being paid a fee for his or her time, he or she should admit that on the stand. Responsible expert witnesses are paid for their *time*, not for their *opinions*.

If I'm Not an Advocate for Children, What Am I?

The pediatrician was being cross-examined in a child physical abuse case. "You're an advocate for children" was the theme.

"Isn't it true you have only testified for the prosecution in these cases?" the defense attorney barked.

"Well," the doctor responded, "I give my opinion to anyone who asks. I can't control who elects to call me as a witness."

"And you are a member of all these professional organizations: the American Professional Society on the Abuse of Children, the California Professional Society on the Abuse of Children," the questioner continued, listing several other professional groups.

"Well, yes. As a professional I try to join good organizations. Would you want I should be a member of a group that advocates *abusing* children?" the witness replied.

"Well, there are other professional organizations," the lawyer began again. "For example, you aren't a member of any organization that advocates on behalf of those who are accused, such as the ACLU, are you?"

"I didn't mention that because it has nothing to do with my professional affiliations," the doctor said slowly, "but as a matter of fact, I am a member of the ACLU, sir. It's just that I don't belong to that organization because of my professional work. I belong simply because I believe that's my obligation as an American."

Expert witnesses should be aware that they become more vulnerable to attack as advocates, rather than objective experts, when the majority of their income is derived from court fees. As one trial judge has urged: "An expert witness should never become solely one party's expert advocate nor a 'gun for hire.' Rather an expert witness should be an advocate for the truth with testimony to help the jury and the Court reach the ultimate truth in a case, which is the basis of any verdict" (*Van Blargan v. Williams Hospitality Corp.*, 1991, p. 248).

It is certainly appropriate for an expert witness to charge a fee for his or her time. The expert witness should be careful that the fee charged is consistent with community standards; typical fees in Fallon, Montana, for example, might not be the same as those charged in New York City. (The setting of fees and related issues are discussed in more detail in Chapter 6.) The expert witness can expect, however, that the charging of fees will be a ripe area for cross-examination.

A witness who spends a considerable amount of professional time working as an expert witness is vulnerable to attack as a biased witness. The opposing side will attempt to show the witness's track record as a "for-hire" witness for one particular party. Although the term *witness* might be used in court, "whore" ("prosecutor whore," "plaintiff whore," or "defense whore"—take your pick) is the clear implication. Indeed, there are some witnesses who are appropriately labeled as such (see the examples discussed in Chapter 7). The frequency with which a witness testifies for a certain side, and for what financial gain, will be used as a measure of his or her objectivity.

Courts have long recognized the legitimacy of cross-examining witnesses by probing their financial interest in the litigation: "Information as to whether a particular expert routinely testifies for a particular category of party is certainly of some value in determining whether he may have a predisposition either to exculpate or find fault" (*Trower v. Jones*, 1988, p. 301).

In facing cross-examination on this issue, the witness should make clear that his or her fees are charged for the *time* involved, not for the opinions given; for example: "I charge $100 an hour for my time, whether it is to review files, discuss the case with the attorneys or testify in court. I charge that same fee whether my opinion is supportive of the client's position or adverse to it." As a practical issue, for any professional to become a full-time professional witness would be ill-advised. In addition to the practical considerations, the credibility of a professional witness is simply too easily assailed. A truly objective witness should be willing to accept and review cases submitted by parties on both sides of a controversy; for example, from both prosecutors and criminal defendants. A professional's opinion should not be swayed by which side of the courtroom he or she will be asked to sit on or marketed to the highest bidder.

❏ Notes

1. This is usually true. But face it, there are just some attorneys who enjoy being nasty all the time—really.

2. There are two caveats to this rule: I have searched for any case anywhere in the United States in which a witness was required to answer yes or no, and I have never found one. It is possible that in some state, the law may impose that requirement. Additionally, although the rules of evidence do not require yes/no responses, that fact might not be appreciated by the trial judge. He or she may nevertheless mandate yes/no responses. The advice that follows in the text is even more significant in those situations.

3. This is an inexcusable form of cross-examination. Unless there are reasons, supported by quality research, to conclude that these are significant factors affecting the professional's judgment, the cross-examiner should not delve into the witness's personal history and/or sexual orientation. Cross-examination, by either side, should be about professional skills and judgment. Personal attacks and insinuation have no place in the cross-examination of a professional.

4. Motions *in limine* are pretrial motions made to the court to limit or prohibit specific questions from being asked and/or particular evidence from being presented.

6

Medical and Mental Health Professionals as Experts in Legal Cases

BENJAMIN E. SAUNDERS

It is not uncommon for medical and mental health professionals to be called upon to serve as expert witnesses or expert consultants in criminal and civil legal proceedings. For professionals who work with certain types of cases, such as victims of domestic violence, persons going through divorce and custody proceedings, child abuse victims, violent crime victims, sexual offenders, head injury patients, and the chronically mentally ill, the likelihood of being asked to serve as expert witnesses or consultants in legal cases is high. Unfortunately, most professionals have had little training or preparation for how to provide such expert services, and have not examined the professional issues surrounding this activity. Graduate and professional school curricula often include some material on legal issues, usually about the legal ramifications of ethical infractions and negli-gent practice. However, they rarely include material concerning the provision of expert services in legal cases. Therefore, medical and mental health professionals most often learn how to deliver these services through "on-the-job" training, professional reading, and occasionally from professional continuing education courses.

The purpose of this chapter is threefold. The first section discusses several important background issues concerning the differing pro-fessional perspectives of attorneys and medical and mental health professionals, and the general roles that experts often are called to fulfill. The second section addresses several ethical considerations associated with expert witness testimony and expert consultation services. The final section presents a few practical guidelines, sug-gestions, or tips for professionals to help them deliver expert services and avoid some of the many pitfalls that await medical and mental health experts who become involved in legal cases.

❏ Differences in Professional Perspectives

Medical and mental health professionals and attorneys need to be familiar with several underlying issues that, if improperly under-stood, can lead to serious problems in the delivery and use of expert services. The professional perspectives of health care professionals and attorneys are different, and the clash of these perspectives can create problems. The delivery of expert services often involves as-suming roles that are unfamiliar to health care professionals and counter to their professional perspectives. At the same time, attor-neys may not understand the ethical and professional limitations that bind medical and mental health experts.

Through professional education, training, practice, and profes-sional acculturation, all professionals develop views of their pro-fessional selves and responsibilities. Medical and mental health professionals generally view themselves as helpers, dedicated to improving the health, mental health, and well-being of their patients. The quality of their practice and their status as professionals are judged by how their patients respond to treatment, and any harm to their patients is viewed as failure.

Health care professionals also view themselves as science based. They rely on scientific findings to guide the assessment and diagnostic techniques, treatments, and interventions they use with their patients. They place a high value on gathering thorough, objective, and scientifically sound data to use in assessing and diagnosing their patients. They use the results of all examination and assessment procedures necessary, consider all the possible explanations for the results found, develop a case formulation, and make a diagnosis based upon all the data available. They then deliver empirically supported treatment based upon the results of the evaluation and diagnostic process.

Attorneys are advocates for a position. Their job is to argue vigorously for their clients' legal position using any methods available that are consistent with the rules of law. Attorneys are side-takers. Their job is to take a side and develop a convincing and persuasive case for the client's stance. Consequently, attorneys look at information associated with a case differently from medical and mental health professionals. They view case information as either helpful or unhelpful to the position of the client. Their task is to emphasize and bolster information that is helpful to the client's case, and to refute, challenge, and minimize information that is harmful. Stated simply, attorneys start out with a position and look for information to support it, whereas medical and mental health professionals examine the information available and see where it leads. Therefore, a fundamental difference exists between the professions that can lead to difficulty when they come together in an expert witness situation.

ROLES OF THE EXPERT

Witness Versus Consultant

Expert medical and mental health professionals most often serve in one of two primary roles, as expert witnesses or as expert consultants. These roles are different, contradictory in many ways, and carry different tasks, responsibilities, and ethical concerns. Frequently, however, the boundary between these two roles can become difficult to discern, raising ethical considerations for experts.

The primary duty of an expert *witness* is to provide the trier of fact (i.e., a judge or jury) with accurate information and objective, unbiased, and impartial opinions about case-relevant issues that are within the expert's specific area of expertise. The hallmark of expert witnesses is impartiality, and their primary obliga-tion is to the court, not to the attorney or client who engaged them. Though expert witnesses typically are hired by one side or the other, their role is that of an unprejudiced educator of the trier of fact, *not* as an advocate for the side that called them. Con-sequently, although expert witnesses should be forceful proponents of their conclusions and opinions, they should not be concerned with the ultimate outcomes of cases.

> *Expert witnesses' primary obligation is to the court, not to the attorney or client who engaged them.*

In contrast, an expert *consultant* has an advocacy duty. In this situation, an expert is hired by an attorney specifically to provide technical and strategic assistance in preparing the case. The expert consultant works with the attorney to examine the case information and to develop strategies for strengthening the client's position and challenging the arguments of the other side. The primary obligation of the expert consultant is to the attorney and client who hired him or her, and in this sense, the expert consultant is an advocate. How-ever, like expert witnesses, expert consultants have an obligation to maintain high scientific, ethical, and clinical standards. Unlike expert witnesses, however, their primary responsibility in a case is to use their professional and technical expertise to help the client develop and win the case.

Obviously, these two roles can be contradictory in their purpose and function. Most professionals would find it difficult to be both impartial and an advocate at the same time. However, it is not uncommon for experts to be asked to fulfill both roles simultane-ously. Therefore, one of the most critical initial tasks of the expert is to develop a clear understanding with the attorney about the expert's specific role in the case, the legal processes involved, the expected tasks of that role, and the ethical issues associated with that role.

As a general rule, an expert should not attempt to fulfill the roles of both expert witness and expert consultant in the same case. Maintaining a proper boundary between the two roles, and knowing when and how to shift gears between them, is simply too difficult. At the very least, serving in both roles gives the appearance of a conflict of interest, and chances are high that a sense of advocacy will creep into the work of developing objective expert opinions. Therefore, the expert should clarify his or her role in a case with the attorney early in the engagement process.

Even when the role of the expert has been designated as that of witness, it is not uncommon for attorneys to ask the expert for strategic advice. When approached in this way, expert witnesses have to make a judgment about whether fulfilling these requests may compromise their objectivity and ability to act as impartial expert witnesses, or constitute the appearance of a loss of objectivity. For example, an attorney may ask an expert witness to develop a set of questions for the cross-examination of an opposing expert that is specifically designed to impeach the expert's credentials, discredit the scientific basis for the expert's opinions, and directly challenge those opinions in a persuasive manner. Developing strategic questions such as these is clearly an advocacy activity, not an educative task. In this example, the attorney is not simply seeking technical or scientific information about a topic; rather, he or she is seeking a script for cross-examination.

Providing strategic advice may affect an expert witness's objectivity. After helping to develop questions calculated to discredit a particular position (that of the opposing expert witness), the expert may find it difficult to consider seriously that position in his or her own expert witness work. After all, the expert has just worked very hard to discredit that position. Consequently, in this example helping the attorney may have the functional effect of limiting the options the expert objectively considers in his or her own testimony, presenting an ethical problem.

On the other hand, some requested activities may be consistent with the objective, impartial, and educative stance of the expert witness. For example, an attorney may ask for aid in interpreting a technical point in a scientific article or request an explanation of different sides of a controversial issue in the field. In these situations, if the expert witness provides the information to the requesting attorney, there is no conflict with the role of expert witness. He or she is simply educating the attorney, not developing case strategy.

It is also appropriate for expert witnesses to discuss with attorneys how best to present their conclusions and opinions to the trier of fact within the rules and conventions of court. Presentation of expert testimony is fundamentally a teaching task. Consequently, expert testimony is an interaction between the unbiased professional/ technical expertise of the witness and the legal expertise of the attorney. If the trier of fact is to benefit from the educative value of the expert testimony, it is appropriate for experts to confer with attorneys about presenting their testimony.

As a guide, experts engaged as witnesses should limit their "consultation" functions to providing objective, educative, or technical information to the attorneys with whom they work. This activity is consistent with their role and does not present a challenge to their impartiality. Expert witnesses should be careful, however, about participating in activities that could be construed as strategic and that may compromise their objectivity.

Functions of the Expert Witness

After it is clear that the expert will serve as a witness rather than a consultant, the expert should then clarify the function he or she will fulfill in the case. Medical and mental health expert witnesses most often serve one of three functions: background witness, case witness, or evaluating witness. These roles are distinguished by how particular to the case and client the expert's opinions are, and by the nature of the information used by the expert to develop his or her opinions.

Expert witnesses most often serve one of three functions: background witness, case witness, or evaluating witness.

Background witnesses provide general scientific background information about basic scientific principles and/or phenomena relevant to a case. They do not express opinions about the specific case. Background witnesses rely on their professional expertise to develop their opinions and usually do not review materials describing the facts of particular cases; such review is unnecessary because these witnesses render opinions only about general scientific issues.

For example, in a child abuse case an expert might be called to give general information about why a child might delay disclosing having been abused. The expert might cite scientific research describing the percentage of children who delay disclosure and for how long. The expert might use clinical case reports and his or her own clinical experience to describe some of the common reasons children delay disclosure and the reasons they ultimately tell. The expert does not have to review case material or assess the child involved in the case to deliver these opinions. This testimony educates the trier of fact about this issue, but is not specific to the case at hand and does not explain why this particular child might have delayed disclosing abuse. Therefore, the expert is simply providing background information that, from the attorney's point of view, "sets the stage" for other parts of the case.

The *case witness* does review information specific to the case, including clinical case records, police reports, witness statements, videotaped interviews, depositions, and other existing case materials. However, this expert will not conduct an independent assessment of the client(s) involved because such examination is unnecessary for him or her to develop opinions about the requested topics. The existing case material provides sufficient information for the expert to develop sound opinions with a reasonable degree of certainty and confidence. The case witness can provide general background information, but he or she can also give opinions that are directly related to the case at hand. Based upon the expert's review of the case materials, he or she can relate the background material to the specific case.

Using the example from above, a case witness would review as much of the available case material as necessary to develop confident opinions about the issue of delayed disclosure. He or she may review clinical progress notes, videotaped interviews, and witness statements in which specific questions were asked of the child about why the child did not tell about the abuse before. The expert witness can evaluate the credibility of this information, relate it to current knowledge about the phenomenon of delayed disclosure, and develop opinions based upon this material.

The *evaluating witness* has knowledge of background information, reviews case material, and conducts an independent assessment of the client who is the subject of his or her opinions. The evaluating witness is able to develop opinions about the case based not only on his or her professional knowledge and experience and the work of others, but also using the results of his or her own evaluation. Therefore, this type of expert can be the most specific in his or her opinions and, likely, the most confident. In the example from above, the evaluating witness would utilize his or her expertise and knowledge of the literature on delayed disclosure, would review the necessary and available case material, and would conduct an examination of the child regarding this issue. The expert would then develop his or her opinions based upon all of this information.

The choice about the expert's functioning as background, case, or evaluating witness should be negotiated by expert and attorney early in the engagement process. However, the expert's role may change as the case progresses. This decision is usually based upon three primary issues: the topics for opinion development requested by the attorney, the nature of the case material available, and the difficulties associated with assessing the client.

The expert who functions as a background witness is usually requested to fill that role by the attorney. In this case the lawyer typically will explain to the expert that he or she is not looking for opinions directly related to the case at hand, but rather is seeking general educational information about a narrow topic. Therefore, the choice of having the expert function as a background witness is usually a straightforward process.

The decision concerning whether the expert will participate as a case or evaluating witness is usually more complicated. Obviously, if the attorney desires opinions that are not general but specific to the case, then the expert will have to examine material related to the case in order to develop those opinions. Three issues then come into play. First, what types of information about the case and about the client does the expert need in order to develop the specific opinions requested? This decision is entirely up to the expert. The expert should have a clear idea about what information he or she will need in order to develop opinions about the requested topics and to have a high degree of confidence in those opinions. For example, an expert may be asked to evaluate whether a child sexually assaulted in a day-care center suffered any psychological harm as a result. It would be up to the expert to determine what information and data he or she requires to develop such an opinion.

The second issue is, What information is currently available? The expert must determine if the information contained in existing case materials and records is sufficient for him or her to develop an opinion and to have a reasonable degree of confidence in that opinion. If the necessary information is available, then gathering additional information (e.g., by examining the client) is unnecessary. However, if the available data do not provide sufficient information for the expert to develop a confident opinion, then the expert will need to gather additional material.

The third issue is, Can additional information be obtained with only a reasonable amount of difficulty and distress? Although it seems intuitive to suggest that gathering more information is always better, obtaining additional case and client information rarely comes without problems. The most obvious problem is the financial cost of obtaining more information, typically through a client examination. Examinations can be expensive. However, conducting examinations and obtaining new information in other ways also present less obvious difficulties. Examinations may cause significant psychological distress to clients as they are called upon to remember, discuss, and defend traumatic events. In child cases, additional interviews of the child may compromise pending criminal cases for either the prosecution or the defense. Gathering collateral information from family members and friends may involve revealing sensitive information to these individuals. Therefore, the need for additional information must be balanced with the costs and difficulties of obtaining the information. Experts must recognize these costs and problems, and must determine whether additional information is necessary to their developing confident opinions, given the potential negative effects to the parties involved.

In the example used above, the expert may determine that the damages to the child from the day-care molestation simply cannot be determined solely through review of existing case and clinical records. Instead, a full psychosocial examination of the child is required for the expert to develop a confident opinion about potential damages. Such an examination necessarily would involve asking the child about the sexual assault experiences; fully discussing the circumstances of the assaults; talking about the child's feelings, thoughts, physical sensations, and memories of the assaults; questioning the child about his or her symptoms; and challenging the child's attributions about all of these issues. Even when skillfully conducted in a sensitive manner, this type of examination can be distressing and upsetting to a child. Therefore, the expert must determine whether the additional information to be gained by interviewing the child is clearly necessary to the expert's development of the desired opinions, given the financial costs and potential for significant distress to the child that may be involved.

❏ **Ethical Issues**

As anyone who has had even minimal contact with the legal system has discerned, it is very complex, with complicated sets of rules and conventions governing the most minute procedures. Possibly because of its complexity, the legal system takes itself very seriously, believing that nearly every other segment of society (particularly that made up of medical and mental health professionals) should drop everything and respond to it immediately when it beckons. To get others to respond, legal professionals use various tools (e.g., notices, subpoenas, court orders). People are always being ordered to do this or that, and commanded to appear here and there, all with the implication that if these directives are not obeyed instantly and without question, dire consequences will come. These directives, coupled with the fundamentally adversarial nature of the legal system, can be intimidating to outsiders. Medical and mental health experts can get caught up in this atmosphere, with its web of orders and intimidation, and feel as if they must do everything directed by any legal practitioner, with little recourse.

When entering the legal profession's house, medical and mental health experts cannot check their own professional ethics, obligations, and practices at the door. The fact that the legal system demands something does not automatically relieve medical and mental

health professionals of their ethical requirements, duties, and obligations. Consequently, just because a lawyer, or even a judge, asks,
demands, or commands that a health care professional do something
does not mean that it must be done without question or that ethical
obligations and clinical standards are automatically abrogated.

Medical and mental health professionals are obliged to follow their
professional codes of ethics, to do no harm to their patients, to
provide the best care and professional services possible, to know the
boundaries of their knowledge and expertise, to know the limits of
scientific knowledge, to maintain standards of confidentiality, to
function in a manner consistent with good and ethical clinical practice, and to avoid conflicts of interest. If complying with the demands
of the legal system will necessitate the breaching of ethical or clinical
standards, health care professionals are obliged to challenge those
demands. Therefore, experts should be aware of the mechanisms
available for contesting potentially compromising demands made by
the legal system.

*Experts cannot rely
on the attorneys
who engaged them
to protect the ex-
perts' professional
and ethical interests.*

At times, the demands of the legal system can blur ethical boundaries, and situations can arise that make following the
ethical course difficult or confusing for experts. In these predicaments, experts cannot rely on the attorneys who engaged
them to protect the experts' professional
and ethical interests. Many attorneys may
not be familiar with the specific ethical
standards of practice for medical and men-
tal health professionals that apply, and cannot be relied upon for
advice. Most important, attorneys are concerned primarily with
winning their clients' cases, not with protecting the experts they hire
from making ethical errors. It is the job of attorneys to use expert
consultation and testimony for the benefit of their clients, and it is
perfectly appropriate for them to attempt to get experts to do and say
things that are most beneficial to their cases. It is the responsibility
of experts to monitor their own work, seek consultation with colleagues when needed, obtain their own legal advice or representation
if required, and ensure that they are functioning in an ethical and
professionally appropriate manner. Therefore, experts must remem-

ber that they are medical and mental health professionals first, with all the ethical obligations of their profession, and experts involved in the legal system second.

CONFIDENTIALITY

Probably the most common ethical problem confronting medical and mental health experts in legal cases concerns client confidentiality. Some professionals might question if the common rules of confidentiality even apply to legal clients, particularly in civil cases. One basis for this position is that clients seen in a legal context simply are not the same as patients seen for clinical purposes, and there is no expectation of confidentiality with these clients. However, ethical codes and state laws governing most health care professions do not contain exceptions for professional work done in the context of legal cases. Particularly for evaluating witnesses, the interaction between experts and legal clients is strikingly similar to what would occur in a clinical context. Consequently, it is likely that legal clients would have an expectation of confidentiality similar to clinical patients. Therefore, the notion that the obligations health care professionals have to legal clients are qualitatively different from those they have with clinical patients is a tenuous proposition.

Another basis for this position is that the rules of discovery abrogate any responsibility for maintaining confidentiality. According to legal discovery rules, both sides in a case are entitled to certain types of information from the other side. This is an example of a situation where there may be a clash between the legal and health care systems. The question is, Just because the legal system says that information can be or even must be revealed, does that automatically relieve medical and mental health professionals of their confidentiality obligation under the rules that govern the health care system? This situation can be generalized to the question, Just because the legal system says that as far as it is concerned health care professionals are allowed to do something, can health care professionals do it regardless of their common ethical standards and clinical practices? The position taken here is, no, they cannot. In general, the ethical standards and practices common to clinical practice should be followed in legal cases.

Therefore, the most conservative approach for experts to take is to consider all information they obtain about specific clients in legal cases as confidential in the same way they would for clinical patients. Confidentiality concerns are most obvious when experts examine clients as part of their information-gathering procedures. Even though such examinations take place as part of a forensic or fact-gathering process that is specifically intended for use in a legal proceeding and is not part of a course of clinical assessment and treatment, the most conservative position would be to assume that the common rules of confidentiality still apply and that clients expect it.

As noted above, there is little reason to believe that state confidentiality laws, professional codes of ethics, and standards of practice do not apply to these cases, even though the assessment procedures are conducted for legal rather than clinical purposes. Therefore, the expert should not release information about the case and the results of the examination to anyone, including the client's attorney, without appropriate release forms being completed by the client or unless there is some other appropriate reason for an abrogation of confidentiality, such as a specific court order directing the expert to release information. The fact that an examination is done in the context of a "legal case" does not suspend the expert's obligation to maintain confidentiality. Consequently, experts should take reasonable measures to ensure that confidentiality is maintained, not to release information about a client except under appropriate conditions, and to obtain informed consent from legal clients before releasing information.

A certain level of confidentiality also applies in cases where the expert reviews only case material and client records, and does not evaluate a client. This situation is comparable to a clinical consultation. For example, if a health care professional were to ask a colleague to consult on a particular clinical case, the colleague would be bound by confidentiality even though he or she had not actually examined the patient or established a clinical relationship with the patient. The consultant likely would give his or her opinions about the case to the requesting professional without a specific release of information, but to no one else. Therefore, even in case review situations, information and opinions should be considered as having a certain level of confidentiality.

However, maintaining confidentiality in legal cases can be difficult and requires planning on the part of experts. Many people are interested in the results of experts' examinations and in their opinions. Defense attorneys, prosecutors, attorneys for other interested parties, guardians *ad litem*, police officers, child protection workers, parties in the case, and even judges may ask experts for reports detailing the results of their examinations. It is not uncommon for those with interests in the case to contact experts by mail, telephone, or even in person and ask for informal summaries of the results and their opinions. In high-profile cases, members of the media may call and ask for information or opinions. Experts confronted with such letters and calls must remember that they are bound by the rules of confidentiality and, therefore, must respond appropriately.

It is not uncommon for callers to respond impatiently and indignantly when experts explain the rules of confidentiality and why they cannot provide the requested information. Callers may attempt to intimidate experts, citing their "right" to the information under the rules of discovery or because of some other legal explanation. Some may threaten experts with sanctions, whereas others may try a more friendly and folksy approach to obtain the information. In these cases, experts should simply explain that they are bound by the standards of confidentiality, but that they will be happy to release the information if the callers provide appropriate release documents signed by the clients, a court order directing the release of the information to them, or some other bona fide mechanism that allows the release of the information. Experts should not be intimidated into breaking their own ethical codes and standards of practice.

Experts may find several practices to be useful in maintaining appropriate levels of confidentiality. First, as noted above, experts should consider that the common rules of confidentiality used in clinical cases also apply to legal cases, and their professional conduct should be guided by this knowledge. Second, experts should ask the attorneys engaging them to obtain appropriate releases of information early in their involvement in a case. Occasionally, experts may have to explain to attorneys that they believe that the rules of confidentiality apply in these situations, even though they are not clinical cases. Release forms usually contain the names of the people to whom information can be released, describe the situations in which information can be released by the expert, and detail the nature of the information that can be released. For example, information usually will need to be given to the attorney engaging the expert and to the opposing counsel. Common situations in which client information will be released include conversations, correspondence, reports, affidavits, depositions, and courtroom testimony. Experts should ask that release forms allow the release of any and all case information obtained by the expert from any source, because they would not want to be restricted in how they can present their opinions. In general, experts should anticipate as best they can situations where client information will need to be revealed and obtain appropriate releases of information.

Third, releases of information should be obtained by experts directly from all persons examined. These releases should be secured in conjunction with the informed consent procedures described below. Fourth, experts should maintain all legal case records in a reasonably secure setting, similar to that provided for clinical case records. Legal cases tend to generate a great deal of paper and other materials, and experts may find themselves housing copies of medical records, depositions, police records, videotapes, and so on. Experts should be able to store this material in a secure place. Finally, experts should train their staff and colleagues concerning confidentiality procedures in legal cases, particularly if media attention is anticipated. Staff and even professional colleagues may not be aware that confidentiality applies to these cases or that procedures used in clinical cases should be followed. Typically, this means that no information about cases should be released by staff or colleagues.

INFORMED CONSENT

The duty to obtain informed consent from clinical patients (and/or their guardians) about interventions is a basic ethical obligation that also applies to legal cases. It is particularly relevant in situations where experts are evaluating clients for legal purposes. Expert examiners should fully inform these clients (and/or their guardians) about several issues, including (a) the professional qualifications of the examiner, (b) the purpose of the evaluation, (c) the role of the expert evaluator, (d) what assessment procedures will be conducted as part of the examination, (e) the risks, if any, associated with the assessment procedures, (f) how the results of the evaluation will be used, (g) to whom the results will be given by the expert, and (h) the anticipated situations in which the information obtained during the examination may be revealed by the expert. Clients should be fully informed of these issues, have the chance to ask questions about them, and have their questions answered satisfactorily before being asked to give their consent to be examined. In general, consent should be obtained in writing. Permission regarding the release of information should be obtained only after the informed consent process has been completed and, preferably, after the examination has been completed.

Several of these issues are discussed routinely with clinical patients, and similar approaches to informed consent can be used in legal cases. For example, it is common for clients not to understand the professional differences among clinical social workers, psychologists, psychiatrists, and other mental health experts. Examiners should explain their professional disciplines and their areas of special expertise. Likewise, medical and mental health professionals routinely explain the risks of assessment procedures to clients. However, some of these issues require special attention in legal cases.

Most important, examiners should explain to clients carefully and thoroughly the purpose of their examinations. Usually this means explaining that the purpose is to gather information and data for the sole purpose of aiding the expert in developing opinions to be used in legal proceedings associated with the case. Experts should explain to clients that legal assessments are not for clinical purposes, and that legal evaluations are not therapy or treatment. These evaluations are not intended to make clients feel better, to improve their functioning, or to help them with their problems. Indeed, legal evaluations may include confronting and challenging clients in ways that would not be done with clinical patients, which has the potential for increasing their distress. Experts should be confident that clients do not view them as therapists, or the legal assessment process as a part of treatment.

Experts acting as expert witnesses should explain to clients that their role is that of objective and impartial examiner who has been asked to develop professional opinions about specific issues in the

*Clients should under-
stand that expert
witnesses are not on
one side or the other.*

case. Clients should understand that expert witnesses are not on one side or the other, even though they may have been hired by one side, and that expert witnesses have no special interest in the outcomes of cases. The expert's role as an objective, impartial, and scientifically based educator of the trier of fact should be explained to the client. Experts should explain to clients that they may serve as witnesses in legal proceedings associated with the case and will use all of the information gathered in the examination as part of the basis for their opinions. Clients should understand that any of the information they give in their assessments may become part of reports, affidavits, or testimony.

The procedures used in the assessment process should be explained to clients so that clients are able to give informed consent to participate. Any risks associated with those procedures should be explained fully, including the potential for psychological distress. For example, if clients will be asked to describe traumatic experiences, they may become upset. Experts may explain to clients that it is the job of the expert to be skeptical and to search for alternative explanations for any problems or difficulties. Consequently, experts may challenge clients on certain points, which may cause clients distress. Experts should explain to clients that they are reviewing case materials as part of the assessment process. This is especially important when a client's medical or mental health records are being reviewed. Experts should be confident that clients understand the assessment procedures to be used and any risks those procedures carry prior to giving consent to participate.

Finally, experts should explain how the assessment results will be used, who will have access to the information from the experts, and in what situations the information will be revealed by the experts. Issues of confidentiality should be discussed at this time as well. Only after clients have been fully informed of these issues should they be asked for their consent, and when consent is obtained, assessment can proceed. Although oral consent may be sufficient in some cases, it is preferable to obtain written consent.

KNOWLEDGE AND EXPERTISE

As expert witnesses, medical and mental health professionals must be cautious not to express opinions that go beyond the scientific knowledge of their fields, comment on issues outside the scope of their personal expertise, or make statements that have only marginal bases in scientific fact, common clinical practice, or their own professional experience. It is not uncommon for experts to be asked or even pressured to skate the boundaries of scientific knowledge, standard clinical practice, and their own expertise when delivering their opinions. This pressure can be overt, but more often it is subtle, gradual, and almost imperceptible. For example, attorneys may ask experts to express their opinions more definitively and with fewer qualifications. Experts may be asked to minimize their acknowledgment and discussion of valid points of controversial issues that do not support attorneys' cases. They may be asked to overgeneralize their opinions to situations to which they do not apply. They may be asked to state their opinions using certain language that has legal importance, but slightly changes the meaning of the testimony.

Experts hired for one purpose may be asked to express opinions about other issues that are related to, but actually beyond, their areas of expertise. When these requests are made, they may appear innocent enough, especially when made in rather informal conversations. But the result is that experts may feel obliged to go just a little too far in their opinions, causing an ethical breach.

There is nothing unethical about experts expressing their opinions forcefully and skillfully, or using legally meaningful language that is consistent with the intent of their testimony. Experts are educators, and helping the trier of fact to understand technically complex ideas and issues is the job of expert witnesses. Indeed, expert witnesses should always be looking for better ways to communicate their ideas and express their opinions in manners that are persuasive to the trier of fact. That is part of their job as educators. It is also not inappropriate for attorneys to help experts convey opinions in ways that are most helpful to their cases.

However, experts should guard against pressure that results in their expressing marginally supportable or incomplete opinions. In their testimony, expert witnesses will be asked not only what their opinions are, but also to explain the factual and scientific bases for their opinions. The standard often cited is that opinions should be held within "a reasonable degree of medical/scientific certainty." Like many legal standards (e.g., reasonable doubt, preponderance of the evidence), this one is not operationally defined in the law, and is open to considerable interpretation by individual experts. However, medical and mental health professionals can use the standards of science and their professions to ensure that the opinions they hold are supportable. In addition, experts must abide by their oath to tell not only the truth, but the whole truth when giving opinions and explaining the supporting bases for their opinions.

For example, suppose there is a genuine scientific or clinical controversy in an expert's field about a certain issue relevant to the case. The expert, using his or her training, experience, and knowledge of the scientific and clinical literature, develops a confident opinion about the controversial issue and how it applies to the case. When asked about the basis for his or her opinion, the expert is obligated to tell "the whole truth," including explaining both sides of the controversial issue and why he or she falls on one side or the other. If the research literature has produced mixed results about an issue, the expert should not cite only those portions of the literature that support his or her opinions. Rather, the expert should describe the different findings in the literature and explain why he or she takes a certain position. Therefore, although experts can work with attorneys to ensure that their opinions are delivered in the most effective manner, they should resist any suggestions that alter the meaning or intent of their opinions, result in the "whole truth" not being told, are not scientifically sound, or are outside their expertise.

CONFLICTS OF INTEREST

Experts should consider whether their participation in particular cases constitutes conflict of interest or the appearance of a conflict. Some conflicts are obvious. For example, if a physician who is paid consultant to a drug corporation working on a new medication is asked by the company to be an expert witness, a conflict of interest exists and he or she should refuse.

Other potential conflicts are not so clear. For example, suppose a particular scientific journal consistently has published articles supporting only one side of a controversial issue, and the journal's editor is called as an expert witness to deliver opinions about that issue. The question would be, Can this person act as an objective, impartial expert in this case, or does his or her past editorial work constitute a conflict of interest?

Probably the most common potential conflict of interest occurs when a medical or mental health professional is asked to serve as an expert witness in a case involving one of his or her clinical patients. Is it appropriate for the professional to do so, and can he or she function in an impartial manner? This is a complicated situation, and the answers depend on several considerations. First and foremost, medical and mental health professionals must consider whether their testifying will have any potential negative effects on their patients, on their relationships with their patients, and on their future treatment of their patients. By testifying as an expert witness, a treating health care professional may be required to say things that could be detrimental to his or her patient's welfare, could harm his or her relationship with the patient, and could hurt his or her ability to provide future treatment. In such a situation, if there is a nontrivial risk of harm to a professional's patients or his or her treatment of patients, the professional should decline to testify as an expert.

Second, health care professionals must ask themselves if they can be objective, impartial expert witnesses in cases involving their patients. After all, medical and mental health professionals develop strong attachments to their patients and often are advocates for them in different arenas. It may be difficult for health care professionals to shift their primary allegiance from their patient to a neutral and unbiased stance. At the very least, there likely is an appearance of a conflict of interest in this situation. Therefore, if a treating health care professional determines that he or she cannot testify in an objective and unbiased manner, or if the professional determines that there is a significant appearance of partiality, he or she should decline to testify as an expert.

Finally, the nature of the testimony to be delivered should be considered. If treating health care professionals simply are going to testify about the facts surrounding their involvement with their patients and their clinical opinions, it is unlikely that conflicts exist. For example, a mental health therapist may be qualified as an expert and then asked to describe his or her assessment and diagnosis of the patient, the nature of treatment delivered, the patient's response to treatment, and other factual issues. The therapist also may be asked about his or her clinical opinions about topics such as the etiology of the patient's problems, the patient's prognosis, problematic behaviors the patient may have exhibited, and even hearsay statements the patient may have made. In this situation, assuming no harm will come to the patient as a result of the testimony, it is unlikely a conflict exists, because the therapist is simply describing the patient's treatment and reporting his or her clinical opinions developed in the role of therapist.

However, what if this same patient is suing a third party for damages resulting from an alleged incident that is a primary subject of the patient's ongoing treatment (e.g., a workplace accident, rape, physical assault, or sexual harassment), and the therapist is asked to deliver expert opinions about the extent of damages specifically attributable to this event? Discerning specific damages is not a typical clinical activity. Therefore, can the therapist be objective and impartial in assessing the credibility of the incident charges and the potential effects specific to the incident, given that he or she has been treating the patient for these problems? Probably not, and a conflict likely exists. Therefore, medical and mental health professionals should consider the nature of the expert testimony requested when asked to serve as experts in cases involving their patients.

Medical and mental health professionals who are asked to serve as expert witnesses in cases involving their own patients should examine each case situation carefully and look for obvious and not-so-obvious conflicts of interest. Ultimately, except in cases of clear conflicts, it is up to experts to determine whether they can act as fair, impartial, and objective examiners in specific cases.

AVOIDING ETHICAL PROBLEMS

At least three mechanisms are available to medical and mental health professionals concerned about ethical problems associated with legal cases. First, they should consult and be familiar with the written codes of ethics that govern their respective professions. Although few codes directly approach expert services in legal cases, potential experts should be aware that the codes apply to these situations as well as clinical practice. Therefore, professionals providing expert services should examine the codes with the activities of expert consultant and witness services in mind, and when they encounter situations that raise ethical issues, they should first read and follow the applicable parts of their codes of ethics.

Second, when potential ethical problems arise, professionals should consult with their respective professional organizations and licensure boards. These organizations may not be as familiar with expert services as with practice issues, and the nature of the ethical problem may have to be explained to them. However, these organizations should be able to provide helpful information and guidance.

Finally, and probably most important, experts should ask for consultation from colleagues, particularly colleagues familiar with the ethical problems encountered in legal cases. Unlike scientific studies, journal articles, and clinical practice, expert services rarely undergo peer review. Most often, experts are simply on their own. Being careful to avoid breaches of confidentiality, experts can help ensure that their work meets ethical, professional, and scientific standards by regularly consulting with respected colleagues about their legal work. Such consultation can help experts avoid unforeseen ethical problems, role conflicts, and potentially embarrassing mistakes in their opinions. Therefore, experts should consider developing an informal peer review mechanism for their legal work.

Experts should consider developing an informal peer review mechanism for their legal work.

❏ Practical Guidelines

Experts can avoid or at least reduce substantially most of the difficulties that arise for them in legal cases if they follow four general principles:

1. Anticipate and try to correct problems before they occur.

2. Communicate clearly and directly with the other professionals involved in the case.

3. Prepare thoroughly and completely.

4. Always keep in mind that they are the experts, and that they alone are responsible for how they conduct their work and for the expert opinions they offer.

Presented below are the common steps involved in expert work, from the initial contact about becoming involved in a case to the final presentation of testimony, along with suggestions about how experts can implement the above-noted principles in order to avoid problems.

INITIAL CONTACTS

Initial contact of a medical or mental health professional about serving as an expert is usually made by an attorney or legal staff. This initial contact sets the tone for how the expert will operate in a case, and being prepared for such initial contacts can help an expert avoid problems in the future. Below are several suggestions about how experts can manage this process.

Find out why they called. The first question an expert should ask of attorneys calling for expert services is why they called him or her in particular. Often, an attorney has learned about the expert from another lawyer, but other paths are common. The attorney may have consulted other medical or mental health professionals who referred him or her to a particular expert, or the attorney may have read something the expert wrote on the subject of interest. Knowing how an attorney chose him or her can give the expert clues about the attorney, the nature of the testimony the attorney is trying to obtain, and hidden difficulties in the case. For example, if the expert knows that colleagues who provide similar expert services referred the attorney, the expert should ask them if they detected any problems with the case that led them not to participate in it.

Find out who the parties in the case are and who they represent. It is important that early in the engagement process the expert understand exactly who the parties are in the case, who the attorney represents, and what the client's role is in the case. Knowing the client and his or her role will help the expert to assess the initial case information provided, anticipate the requests that might be made in the future, and understand for whose interests the attorney will be working. The expert also can use this information to screen for potential conflicts of interest or other difficulties.

Know that this is an audition. During initial contact, the attorney is trying to assess the expert and how helpful he or she might be to the attorney's case. It is likely that the attorney got the expert's name from another attorney and has already done a bit of investigating to learn more about him or her, about his or her past work as an expert and past testimony. The attorney may have obtained transcripts of the expert's past depositions or courtroom testimony before calling. In the initial contact, the attorney wants to learn more about basic issues, such as the expert's professional qualifications and credentials, professional expertise in the area for which witness or consultation services are needed, past cases on which the expert has worked, other attorneys with whom the expert has worked, the expert's availability on certain dates, fees, and so on. In addition, the attorney is evaluating more intangible qualities, such as the expert's "presence" when speaking, demeanor and temperament, physical appearance, articulateness and persuasiveness, command of the subject matter being discussed, layperson's knowledge of applicable legal issues, and any indications that he or she will develop an opinion favorable to the attorney's case. Therefore, initial contact is somewhat like an audition.

Know that the spin doctor is in. In addition to auditioning the expert, the attorney wants to recruit him or her to the attorney's way of thinking about the case. It is likely that the attorney will present the case in a way that is most favorable to his or her viewpoint. In doing so, he or she may describe key information incompletely or omit it altogether, may present only one side of an issue, and may question the credibility and motivations of opposing witnesses while assuming that favorable witnesses are completely truthful. Therefore, the expert should remain skeptical when listening to an attorney describe a case for the first time, and should constantly remind him- or herself that there are at least two sides to this dispute. There is almost always more to the story than is presented initially by an attorney. Therefore, in these early contacts the expert should ask as many questions as necessary to determine as much about the case as possible and to separate facts from spin.

Find out what the issues in question are. During the initial contact, the expert should determine the specific issues for which the attorney is looking for expert help. This may require substantial discussion, because the expert's perspective on the issues involved may be different from that of the attorney. Also, the expert may have ideas about related issues or information that is new to the attorney. Therefore, clarification of the exact topics of the needed expert services is usually an interactive process. Next, the expert should determine if it is possible for him or her to develop confident opinions about those topics. At times, attorneys may request expert opinions or consultation on topics for which there is simply no scientific or clinical basis for opinion. In such cases, experts should explain this to the attorneys and decline to participate in these cases.

Determine whether the expert is really an expert in the area at issue. After clarifying the issues and determining that there is a sufficient basis for expert service, the expert should consider carefully whether or not he or she is really an expert on those issues. Is it his or her primary area of specialization? Does the expert regularly work with these types of cases? Is the expert familiar with the full research and clinical literature on the topic? Is he or she aware of the controversies surrounding the topic? Does the expert know how to conduct the procedures necessary to develop a confident opinion? Nothing is more uncomfortable for an expert witness than being deposed or cross-examined on a topic about which he or she knows something, but is frankly not a true expert. A professional should not hesitate to turn down a case if it does not fall into his or her area of expertise and specialization. It is usually best not to participate in such a case;

instead, the professional should refer the attorney to a colleague who is truly an expert in that area.

Determine what the expert's role will be. During the initial contacts, the expert should determine what services the attorney is looking for and what the expert's role in the case will be. The first issue is whether the expert will act as a consultant or expert witness. This is a critical determination that should be made early in the process. If the expert is to act as a witness, he or she should discuss with the attorney the limits that places on the provision of consultant services. As noted above, the attorney may not understand the ethical problems of an expert's providing both witness and consultant services, and this matter should be resolved early in the process. If the expert is to act as a witness, he or she should discuss with the attorney the issues for which the expert will have to develop opinions, with an eye to understanding whether he or she will be called as a background, case, or evaluating witness. The expert should be able to provide the attorney with a general idea of the limits of his or her opinions in the three roles. It is not uncommon for the expert's role to change as a case progresses. For example, someone initially retained as an expert witness may become a consultant, or a background witness may be asked to become a case or evaluating witness. However, at any point in time, the expert and the attorney should have a clear understanding of what the expert's role is.

Find out if there is enough case information available. During the initial contacts, the expert should find out the nature of the case material and information that will be available, including persons who could be evaluated. The expert should then make a preliminary determination about whether there is sufficient information available for him or her to do the necessary work. In some situations, important case information may not exist or may be inaccessible for some reason, making it impossible for the expert to develop confident opinions.

Remember who is the expert. In all initial interactions with the attorney, the expert should make it clear that he or she will determine what needs to be done to develop the opinions requested and fulfill the role requested. The expert should always remember that role, and should know what he or she needs to do to assess a situation and develop a confident opinion. The expert should resist any attempts to influence how he or she will go about the work needed or to limit his or her access to case records or the clients involved. If attorneys or others place limits on what the expert can and cannot do that make it difficult for the expert to develop confident opinions, he or she should strongly consider not participating in the case.

Supply an updated and accurate résumé or curriculum vitae. The attorney will request a résumé or curriculum vitae from a prospective expert. Prior to sending either to an attorney, the expert should make sure that it is up-to-date and, above all, accurate. If the expert is acting as a witness, the résumé or CV will be provided to the opposing side, and portions of it will likely be investigated. Inaccuracies on a résumé can be embarrassing and can reduce an expert's credibility. The expert should critically examine the résumé line by line, making sure that it is correct. Are the professional organization memberships listed up-to-date? Are all of the educational and professional qualifications accurate? Are the references for professional presentations and writings correct? Is the work history complete and accurate?

Settle the terms of work. Issues such as the expert's availability on certain dates, fees, expenses, retainers, billing practices, and anticipated activities should be discussed and resolved during the expert's early contacts with an attorney. Any limits on the work, such as number of allowed hours or expenses, should be discussed and settled. These issues should not be left hanging or ambivalent, as this will cause problems later. All details should be thoroughly discussed and mutually agreed upon early in the process.

Get it in writing. After the initial contact, an attorney will often ask an expert for copies of his or her résumé or CV and a fee schedule. When providing these items, the expert will find it useful to include a letter detailing his or her terms for acting as an expert in the given case. This letter should list fees, billing practices, retainer requirements, and policies about any special issues. It should explain clearly and explicitly all of the expert's terms for expert services. Such a letter makes for clear communication with the attorney and memorializes the expert's terms in the case record. Once the terms of service and other logistical issues have been settled, the expert should request an engagement letter from the attorney. In this letter the attorney should detail the activities requested and acknowledge the arrangements agreed upon for fees, billing, and other terms of the work. Having all of these decisions in writing will minimize problems later.

Make the financial arrangements. Setting expert fees can be uncomfortable for medical and mental health experts because these services are unlike their usual clinical practices and they may not have much experience with how much to charge and how to collect fees. Many experts have different fee levels for different services. For example, some experts may charge certain fees for activities they can do in their offices, such as reviewing case records and materials, report writing, and attorney consultation, and may have another fee level for client evaluation. If travel is involved, they may charge higher fees for travel time that takes them away from their offices. Most experts probably charge their highest fees for time spent in depositions and courtroom testimony. In setting fee levels, the expert should consider asking colleagues with similar qualifications how much they charge for various expert services. Some professional organizations also offer guidelines for setting expert fees. Whatever fees an expert charges, they should be understood and agreed to by the engaging attorney.

The expert should be clear on the services to be charged for. In general, any time spent doing any activity associated with the case should be billed, including telephone conversations with attorneys about the case. Billing arrangements should be agreed to as well. Time spent on a case may be billed on a monthly, quarterly, or other basis. The terms for billing, such as when payment is expected and whether there will be additional charges for late payments, should also be clear and agreed to from the beginning.

The expert may also consider requiring a retainer, or payment in advance, before beginning work on a case, for his or her protection. The retainer is kept by the professional and services provided are billed against the retainer. If total charges are less than the retainer at the end of the case, the excess amount is returned. Retainers ensure that the expert will be paid for the work done and simplify the billing and collecting process. They are commonly used in the legal profession, and a request for a retainer will come as no surprise to an attorney. The expert should negotiate the size of the retainer with the engaging attorney. For example, the expert may ask for advance payment for 10 hours of work at the negotiated fee or may request a specific dollar amount.

It is not uncommon for there to be some confusion about who is responsible for paying the expert's bill, so this too should be negotiated and put in writing in the engagement letter. In general, the expert should require that the law firm hiring him or her, not the client, be responsible for paying the bill. Again, this is for the expert's protection. Persons, government agencies, insurance companies, or others that the attorney represents may balk at or be slow in paying an expert's bill, and the expert may not even be aware of it, because he or she has never met these other parties—the expert has dealt only with the attorney in the case. In such a situation an attorney may claim inability to pay the expert because the client has not paid the attorney. The expert's anticipating such problems early in the process and making arrangements for the engaging law firm to be responsible for paying the bill can avoid difficulties.

GATHERING INFORMATION AND DEVELOPING OPINIONS

After the initial contacts have been completed and the expert has been engaged, the process of collecting information about the case begins. In this phase the expert sets out to gather the information needed to develop confident expert opinions. Thorough preparation is necessary, and it is the responsibility of the expert to obtain and review all the information he or she needs to develop opinions. For nearly all expert work, with the possible exception of acting as a background witness, this task requires careful review and consideration of the relevant case material available. Depending on the nature of the case, materials reviewed may include medical records, school records, work records, agency records, organizational policies, police reports, witness statements, affidavits, correspondence, depositions, reports, and/or videotaped or audiotaped interviews. Depending upon the issues to be examined and the information available, the expert may need to evaluate the client as part of the information-gathering process. In addition, the expert may need to conduct collateral interviews with others, such as the client's family members, coworkers, teachers, and friends. The expert may need to examine the relevant scientific and clinical literature, and may need to consult with colleagues. As the expert approaches the information-gathering stage, the following suggestions may be helpful.

Have an idea what to look for prior to reviewing materials. Given the nature of the opinions to be developed, the type of case, and the information available, experts should enter the information-gathering stage with distinct ideas about what information they need to have in order to develop confident opinions. Experts may find it helpful to develop outlines of the specific questions they will be asking about the information reviewed, prior to beginning their review.

For example, if an expert in a civil liability case is asked to develop opinions about the likelihood that a child victim of abuse might develop a particular mental or emotional disorder, he or she should have a specific set of questions about predictive factors to assess prior to beginning the information-gathering process. The expert likely would consult the scientific and clinical literature on the long-term effects of child abuse and carefully examine studies that determine the characteristics that tend to be associated with the disorder of interest. The expert may also review his or her own clinical experience concerning these factors and consult with colleagues about this issue. From these sources of information, the expert can develop an outline of the information he or she will need to develop confident opinions. These *a priori* questions will help the expert in making decisions about what documents need to be reviewed, which will not be helpful, and whether a client assessment is necessary. Therefore, experts should spend time determining what information they absolutely need to know to develop the requested opinions and plan the information-gathering process.

Review what is necessary to form opinions. Experts should review all materials relevant to the development of their opinions. It is the expert's responsibility to determine the information needed and to request the relevant documentation. Experts should not rely on attorneys to determine what they should review; this task is up to the experts. Attorneys may not be familiar with the nature of the information experts need to see in particular cases and may not know to supply the pertinent documentation. Also, experts cannot ignore the possibility that attorneys may not supply them with materials believed to be damaging to their cases.

Experts should be active in requesting the materials they need, not simply passive recipients. This process is often interactive. As experts review materials, they often become aware of other documents that may be relevant because they are referred to in the materials reviewed. Experts then should request to see the referenced materials. In addition, as they review materials, experts may determine that some key information they require to develop their opinions is not contained in the materials reviewed or is inadequate. In such situations, experts should ask attorneys and other parties involved in the case if the information is available in other materials or from other sources. If so, it should be acquired.

In gathering information, an expert must become very familiar with the facts and information associated with the case. The expert's command of the facts of a case is often a key element used by triers of fact in determining the expert's credibility and expertise, and thus the weight to assign to the expert's testimony in decision making. Opposing counsel may attempt to reduce the impact of expert testimony by asking the expert questions about obscure facts or issues unfamiliar to the expert, thus implying that the expert has not done a thorough job and has not considered all the information available. Therefore, if experts want their opinions to be taken seriously by triers of fact, they should understand and remember as much information about the case as possible. This can be accomplished only through hard work and time spent reviewing and re-reviewing material about the case. Some experts develop their own outlines, timelines, and/or case summaries to help them organize the facts of the case. Whatever tools an expert uses, thorough and complete preparation is crucial.

As experts sift through the materials available, they may encounter contradictory information about factors critical to their opinions. Experts need to determine if they believe one side or the other of the contradictory information and, most important, the basis for their decisions. An expert should have a reasonable and supportable rationale for why he or she accepts one version of the facts of a situation and rejects another. If no reasonable basis exist for that decision, the expert should be cautious in relying on that information.

Review primary documents. Experts should review the most primary documents available. For example, a medical expert may review an evaluation report from a previous examination. In that report, the examining physician may describe the results of an even earlier examination conducted by another doctor. The expert in this case should not rely exclusively on the secondhand report of the examining physician. Rather, he or she should obtain and review copies of the original medical record describing the initial examination.

Make sure copies are complete. Experts should take steps to ensure that they have complete copies of all materials reviewed. Copying errors do occur, and experts should pay attention to page numbers and to materials that appear to be incomplete. At times, an attorney may indicate that only portions of medical records or depositions are relevant to the issues that are the subject of the expert's opinion and that the expert need only review these portions. This practice may be suggested as a time- and cost-saving measure for all concerned. Experts should be cautious when examining partial copies, however, because relevant information may be contained in the unreviewed portions of the materials. An expert's credibility can be successfully challenged if opposing attorneys point this out in deposition or cross-examination. Therefore, in most situations experts should examine complete copies of all materials.

Ask for other available materials that might be useful. Based upon an outline of necessary information, the expert should ask the attorney if certain materials are available or if certain information is available in other materials. The expert should also be familiar with potential challenges to his or her opinions and should ask for any materials and information that might exist that could be used to challenge those opinions, the basis for the opinions, or the accuracy of the materials and information relied upon in developing opinions.

Again, the expert should be an active seeker of information, not a passive recipient.

Determine if a client evaluation is necessary. For most medical and mental health experts, a pivotal decision in the information-gathering process is whether or not a client examination is necessary for the expert to acquire the information needed to develop confident opinions. The decision that a client evaluation is required for the development of a confident opinion rests solely with the expert. As noted above, this decision is dictated primarily by the match between the information required to develop the requested opinions and the quantity, quality, and nature of the data available from sources other than the client. It is up to the expert to determine if the information available is adequate or not and whether or not it can be obtained from a client examination.

However, the decision actually to conduct such an examination depends on several factors. Other issues must be considered, such as the potential negative impact of an examination on the client, client cooperation, time, cost, and unintended legal consequences. For example, conducting an examination may open the client to examination by experts on the other side of the dispute. Therefore, the expert should determine as early as possible in the information-gathering process whether a client examination will be necessary, and consultation with the attorney about this decision is appropriate.

Consider all alternatives when developing opinions. Experts should work diligently to consider all options and alternative explanations when developing opinions. All professionals tend to have biases about controversial issues in their respective fields, and experts are no exception. That is why some issues are controversial. In legal cases, experts should not automatically, in knee-jerk fashion, espouse their usual opinions on issues for which there may be reasonable competing positions in the field. Rather, carefully, and in good faith, they should consider all alternatives in their opinions, even unpopular ones and ones with which they usually do not agree. Experts should develop conscientiously the bases for their opinions, explaining why they give particular weight to certain materials or facts and not to others, and why they accept specific positions and reject others.

Genuine consideration of all reasonable possibilities is the hallmark of the objective, impartial expert.

Write reports in laypersons' language. Experts often are asked to express their opinions and the basis for their opinions in written reports. Medical and mental health experts should remember that the consumers of these reports usually are not other health care professionals. Therefore, they should write such reports in language that lay readers will understand. The reports should be concise, to the point, and free of professional jargon. When the professional finds it necessary to use technical terms or concepts, these should be explained so that a layperson can understand them. Usually, written reports should be brief, conveying the essence of the expert's opinions and their basis. Details of the supporting facts, information, and decision-making process usually are better left to other forums, such as depositions and testimony.

Genuine consideration of all reasonable possibilities is the hallmark of the objective, impartial expert.

PREPARATION FOR DEPOSITION OR TESTIMONY

After an expert has developed his or her opinions and possibly expressed these opinions in the form of a written report, attention turns to the preparation of the witness for depositions and courtroom testimony. The following are suggestions to help experts cope with these situations.

Know why you believe what you believe. For the expert, describing the substance of his or her opinions under questioning usually is the easy part of giving depositions or courtroom testimony. When questioned, experts may go on and on, expressing broad opinions about many issues. Inexperienced experts are sometimes shocked when opposing attorneys and triers of fact do not simply accept their opinions at face value because of their professional qualifications or standing in their fields. Rather, after hearing experts' opinions, attorneys will ask them to explain the bases for their opinions and why they hold those opinions and not others. Much of their questioning will be devoted to challenging the bases for the experts' opinions, factually, scientifically, clinically, or even personally. Simply put, examining attorneys will question experts about three areas: (a) What is your opinion about the issues you examined? (b) What is the basis for your opinion? (c) What did you rely on to develop the opinion? Competent experts should be well prepared to answer these three questions.

The expert must know why he or she holds particular beliefs and must be prepared to express the basis for those opinions. On what facts did the expert rely? Why did the expert find certain facts credible and not others? On what materials did the expert rely to obtain these facts? Why did the expert review some materials and not others? Why did the expert believe one person and not another? What scientific research supports the expert's position? How does the expert explain studies that appear to contradict his or her opinion? Is the expert's position the prevailing one in his or her profession? Attorneys will ask these and other potentially more hostile questions to dissect the basis for the expert's opinions. Therefore, the expert should be well prepared not only to express opinions, but to defend why he or she holds them and the process used to develop them.

Know why you don't believe what you don't believe. This suggestion is simply the flip side of the preceding suggestion, but equally important. Experts should be able to demonstrate that they considered many options in developing their opinions, and to defend why they rejected competing opinions. The expert should be prepared to answer questions similar to those above about why he or she does not hold competing opinions.

Help the attorney develop direct examination questions that fully present your opinions. Expert witnesses are educators of the trier of fact. Consequently, presenting their opinions in a clear and complete manner is the most critical task for experts. Unfortunately, experts are not allowed simply to give speeches in court. They are limited to answering the questions presented to them by the attorneys. Therefore, experts should work with the attorneys conducting their direct examinations to develop questions that allow them to put their opinions before the trier of fact accurately, clearly, and completely.

Explore creative ways of communicating your opinions. Experts should consider using creative ways to communicate their opinions effectively. Expert witnesses fundamentally are teachers, and they often must try to communicate technically difficult information to lay audiences. The expert should consider using audiovisual aids such as slides, overhead projections, enlarged charts, videotapes, and computer technology if they will help the trier of fact better understand the opinions. Fancy media are no substitute for well-constructed opinions, however, and experts should make sure that the media used do not distract from their messages. However, there are times when these tools can be helpful in communicating complex opinions.

Anticipate likely lines of questioning on cross-examination. Prior to depositions or testimony, experts should consult with the attorneys with whom they work about ways they might expect opposing attorneys to question them on cross-examination. In particular, experts should anticipate ways that opposing attorneys will challenge their opinions, the bases for their opinions, the reasoning they used to arrive at their opinions, and the facts and materials they relied on to achieve those opinions. Assuming that an expert has considered all reasonable opinions and has a sound rationale for his or her opinions, answering these challenges should be straightforward.

Attorneys also can help experts foresee any trial techniques that opposing attorneys might use to contest or even mischaracterize their opinions. Attorneys may be familiar with the styles or techniques commonly used by the opposing lawyers and can work with the experts on ways to manage these techniques. Ultimately, however, the best defenses against any trial technique or "trick" are true expertise; scientifically and clinically sound, impartial, and objective opinion; and thorough preparation.

> *The best defenses against any trial technique are true expertise, impartial opinion, and thorough preparation.*

DEPOSITIONS AND COURTROOM TESTIMONY

Depositions and courtroom testimony are nervous times under the best of conditions. Below are several suggestions that can help experts keep on track during experiences that can be quite anxiety provoking.

Remember, you are an objective, impartial expert. Legal proceedings are adversarial by nature, and it is natural for expert witnesses to get caught up in the spirit of the competition and want to help "win" the case for the side that engaged them. However, the key to credible and useful expert witness testimony is the expert's remembering that he or she is an objective and impartial educator of the trier of fact. It is not the witness's responsibility to "win" the case or be invested in the outcome—that is the job of the attorney. Beyond the fact that maintaining an impartial approach is the ethical thing to do, doing so also increases the witness's credibility with the trier of fact and boosts the impact of his or her testimony. A good guideline is to remember that an expert's opinions and testimony should be the same no matter which side is paying the expert.

Your job is to answer fully the questions asked. Expert witness testimony is actually very easy. The expert simply answers the questions that are asked. It is not the witness's job as an expert to ask the right questions, that is the job of the attorney. It is the expert's job to answer questions as clearly, accurately, and completely as possible.

Listen carefully to the questions asked. In order to answer a question properly, an expert must listen to the exact wording of the question asked. It is not uncommon for an expert to anticipate a question and misunderstand the meaning of the actual question asked by the attorney. The witness should listen carefully to the exact wording of the question asked by the attorney, concentrate on understanding it, and answer what was actually asked, not what the witness thinks the attorney might have meant. If the expert does not understand a question, he or she should ask for clarification or to have it rephrased. It is often useful for the expert to restate the question in his or her answer. For example, an expert may respond to an unclear question by saying, "I am not exactly sure what you mean by that, but if you are asking . . . ." With this type of answer, the expert ensures that he or she is answering the question as he or she understands it.

Always be cautious, conservative, and qualified in expressing opinions. Medical and mental health experts usually should express their opinions in a cautious and conservative manner, with appropriate qualifications. Unqualified, absolute statements using words such as *always, never, must,* and *should* are red flags and should be avoided for several reasons. First, they rarely are accurate. Most issues in medicine and mental health are based on probabilities, risk ratios, and frequencies, and nearly all phenomena have exceptions and qualifications. Therefore, absolute and definitive statements are usually factually wrong. Second, triers of fact are suspicious of absolute statements. Most laypersons know that few things are absolute and unqualified, and definitive statements sound like exaggerations and posturing to them. If they feel an expert witness is improperly inflating his or her opinions, they will give less weight to the expert's testimony or just not believe it at all. Therefore, a cautious, conservative, and properly qualified presentation of opinions actually is more powerful than absolute and definitive statements. Such a presentation also conveys a sense of impartiality, attention to detail, careful consideration, and professionalism to the trier of fact.

Correct attorneys when they improperly characterize your opinions. During examination, an attorney may characterize the expert witness's prior testimony in certain ways, or even repeat it back to the expert prior to asking the next question. The expert should listen to these comments carefully and make sure his or her opinions are not misstated, mischaracterized, or incorrectly interpreted by the attorney. If they are, the witness should correct the attorney prior to answering any further questions.

Do not accept restrictions or limitations on your answers from attorneys. Though it does not happen often, an attorney may attempt to limit the type of answer an expert witness can give to a question. The attorney may offer a menu of answers for the witness to choose from, none of which properly captures the response he or she wants to give. For example, an attorney may ask an expert witness to answer a complex question with only a yes or a no. In such a circumstance, the expert should respond that he or she cannot answer the question with those restrictions and then proceed to answer it in the way he or she would like. If the attorney interrupts the answer, stops the witness, or insists that the question be answered as he or she has requested, the witness can turn to the judge and say, "Your Honor, I took an oath to tell the truth and the whole truth in my answers. I cannot properly tell the whole truth by answering within these restrictions." It is the rare judge who will not allow a witness to answer the question fully under those conditions.

Remember, you are educating the trier of fact, not the attorneys. The expert witness's testimony should be directed to the jury or judge, not the attorneys conducting the examination. For example, the expert should use layperson's language and avoid professional or legal jargon. If the expert must use technical terms, he or she should explain them in lay terms in a teaching manner, avoiding any hint of condescension. The expert should try to use everyday examples and common analogies to explain his or her opinions, and should speak to the jury when answering questions, making eye contact with individual jurors when possible. Most of all, the expert should remember that he or she is there to educate the trier of fact, not the attorneys conducting the examination.

❏ Conclusion

Medical and mental health professionals will continue to participate in legal cases as experts, and those who do need to be aware of the differences in professional perspectives between lawyers and health care professionals. Health care professionals should be attentive to the different roles they can play as experts in legal cases and the potential conflicts between those roles. Legal cases carry the same ethical obligations as clinical cases, though the implementation of ethical principles may be unfamiliar and confusing. Finally, medical and mental health professionals should develop effective techniques to help them fulfill their roles, manage the ethical issues that arise, and be effective witnesses.

7

Cross-Examining the Irresponsible Expert Witness

Experts whose opinions are available to the highest bidder have no place testifying in a court of law.

Judge Patrick E. Higginbotham,
In Re Air Crash Disaster at New Orleans, LA, 1986

As wise as Judge Higginbotham's words are, they have not become universally accepted. Instead of barring questionable expert testimony, most trial judges admit this evidence and permit jurors to assign to it whatever value they deem appropriate. This "let it all in" philosophy is based on the belief that jurors can properly assess the credibility of expert witnesses and will give their testimony the weight it deserves.

This posture creates enhanced responsibilities for the attorney: If jurors' evaluation of expert testimony is to be meaningful, attorneys bear the burden of identifying and exposing irresponsible expert witnesses. This chapter explores how that task might best be accomplished.

❏ **The Damage That Can Be Done
by the Irresponsible Expert Witness**

   Nothing should be more infuriating to an attorney than the en-
trance into a case by an irresponsible expert witness. Assume a case
of child sexual abuse: Envision a young child witness who has had
the courage to testify before her abuser and has been strong in the
face of cross-examination. Her care providers have been supportive
and appropriate, the investigators have done their jobs well, and the
medical personnel and other professionals have performed their
tasks with efficiency and have come to court to share their opinions.
Then into the fray comes some out-of-town professional witness to
offer her standard criticisms about the failures of the investigation,
the inadequacies of the professionals or the fallacies of child witnesses in general, not one of whom the "expert" has ever met.
   When everyone involved in a case has done his or her job well, but
the case is jeopardized by a "for-hire" expert, the opposing attorney
should be angry. When the critiques are recycled boilerplate arguments, the attorney should be furious. When the arguments are
inconsistent with the accepted state of the literature, counsel should
be outraged. That outrage must be turned to motivation. The response of the attorney must be to use knowledge and research to
mount a pointed, professional attack on the irresponsible expert
witness for hire.

❏ **Who Is the Irresponsible Expert?**

   "If you build it, they will come," whispered the voice from the
heavens in the movie *Field of Dreams.* The irresponsible expert witness
might best be identified by those who practice in the *Courtroom of
Dreams,* where the whisper is "If you pay them, they will come."
   Courts across the country have recognized the existence of the
"expert for hire." Some judges have had the courage to prohibit such
witnesses from testifying before a jury. One court rejected a proposed
expert who "offers his services as an expert witness to the [local] Bar,

with a mass mailing every other year" (*Van Blargan v. Williams Hospitality Corp.*, 1991, p. 249); another court refused to allow one to testify who "did not have bona fide qualifications . . . [who] was not involved in independent research . . . but rather was approached to undertake research by an interested party with an interest in the outcome of the research" (*State v. Swan*, 1990, p. 656).

Some well-known trial lawyers have recognized the desire for the professional expert. "If I got myself an impartial witness, I'd think I was wasting my money," one prominent civil attorney has acknowledged (Specter, 1987, p. Z10).

The irresponsible expert is frequently driven by financial interests. However, many experts are also motivated by ego or their own professional or personal agendas to enter the litigation wars.

Before an attorney makes the decision to challenge an opposing expert, he or she should consider carefully what the expert has said. Just because the witness's opinion is adverse to the lawyer's does not necessarily mean the expert is wrong. If an expert provides an opinion adverse to one party, the attorney's first response should be to reconsider whether his or her original position is correct. Even the most adversarial of trial lawyers has the obligation to evaluate an opposing opinion fairly to determine if indeed it might be accurate. Only if the trial lawyer believes that the opposing expert is wrong should he or she develop a confrontational cross-examination strategy.

❏ How to Identify and Expose the Irresponsible Expert Witness

A trial attorney should consider three sets of questions when reviewing opposing expert testimony:

- Is this person qualified? What is the witness's level of training, knowledge, and expertise?
- Is the evaluation process properly done? To what extent has the expert adequately utilized proven processes and procedures, relied upon ap-

propriate studies and research, and made logical conclusions based upon facts and information available?

- Has the witness remained objective and unbiased? Is the witness an expert, or an advocate in expert's clothing?

IS THIS PERSON QUALIFIED?

As I have discussed in Chapter 2, the standard for qualifying as an expert witness is exceptionally minimal. Judges generally allow the jury to decide what value to place on a particular witness's testimony. The weight of that evidence should be significantly influenced by the qualifications of the expert. The cross-examining attorney, then, has the obligation to explore exactly how much expertise the expert witness truly possesses. This starts with a thorough review of the expert's qualifications. A skeptic's approach to examining the expert's curriculum vitae is recommended.

> *The cross-examining attorney has the obligation to explore exactly how much expertise the witness truly possesses.*

Conducting a thorough review of a witness's qualifications takes time. Accordingly, the cross-examining attorney should attempt to identify potential expert witnesses and obtain their curricula vitae as soon as possible.

Identifying expert witnesses is significantly easier in civil than in criminal cases. The rules of discovery in both types of cases require identification of expert witnesses. However, in criminal cases there is frequently no penalty for late disclosure of an expert witness by the defendant.

There are methods that will help the trial attorney determine the identity of opposing expert witnesses prior to receiving formal notice. In some jurisdictions, an indigent criminal defendant must give notice to the state if he or she seeks public funds to hire an expert. This obviously puts the prosecution on notice as to the identity of a potential expert witness. At this hearing, the prosecution should demand a copy of the expert's curriculum vitae. In other jurisdictions, indigent defendants are allowed to move *ex parte* for an order to obtain funds for expert witnesses. Although that application may be made without formal notice to the prosecutor, the motion may nevertheless be filed with the court. Prosecutors should periodically

"Why do I have the feeling that this is a fictitious résumé?"

© by Tom Cheney.

check court files to see if defendants have made such applications. Frequently, requests for funds are supported by the curricula vitae of the proposed expert witnesses.

Most expert witnesses will provide counsel with copies of their curricula vitae. The opposing side should ask for experts' CVs as early in the process as possible. If these documents are not forthcoming, they should be demanded through pretrial motion. A curriculum vitae, or at least a summary of the witness's qualifications, can be mandated in pretrial discovery (see Federal Rules of Criminal Procedure 16[b][1][C]). If a witness has been identified but no curriculum vitae has been provided, the opposing side should not overlook taking the initiative to obtain one: He or she should call the witness directly and ask for one to be mailed.

Once the current CV is obtained, the cross-examining attorney must spend a few hours with it and the cross-examiner's best friend: the telephone. The cross-examining attorney should not assume the accuracy of the witness's curriculum vitae. If the expert lists a particular advanced degree, the attorney should telephone the institution cited and verify it; if the witness lists membership in a particular professional organization, the attorney should obtain a membership list and verify it. Every professional credential should be authenticated. Some cross-examining attorneys may be surprised at how frequently CVs list information that is inaccurate or outdated (see the example provided in Chapter 2).

There are many other items on the curriculum vitae the cross-examining attorney should check:

- *Degrees obtained:* The attorney should substantiate the degrees and internships listed. Some educational programs listed may involve schools that are not accredited or are merely mail-order "diploma factories." College transcripts may be obtainable—these provide the attorney with a close look at exactly how many courses the witness has taken that really focused directly on the witness's claimed area of specialty.

- *Licensure:* A call to a licensing board can verify whether what is stated in the CV is accurate.

- *Articles written:* The attorney should attempt to obtain copies of the articles listed. How many were published in peer review journals?

- *Lectures and/or workshops provided:* The attorney might want to obtain materials from these presentations and compare what the witness teaches his or her colleagues to what he or she states in court.

The attorney should also seek to obtain as many of the witness's prior CVs as possible, to examine what has changed. Sometimes extra credentials appear that should raise flags of concern; other times, credentials mysteriously disappear. For example, an old CV may list an article as "submitted for publication," although a later CV may have no mention of it. A likely conclusion is that the article that was listed as "submitted for publication" was not accepted. The attorney might want to inquire about this on cross-examination. If the journal to which the article was submitted is a peer review journal, the attorney might want to try to obtain, either indirectly or through a motion for discovery, the comments of the expert's peers who reviewed and then rejected the article. This can be powerful testimony

---

What the Expert Is Not

What follows is an excerpt from a trial transcript of the cross-examination of a proposed expert intended to establish a lack of qualifications:

Question: Is there something called board certification in your field?
Answer: Yes, there is.
Question: What does that mean, sir?
Answer: It means that if you have finished your training in a particular specialty in an approved training program and, in addition, you have been in the field, in practice, for two years, then if you want you can take an examination that is called a board examination. It consists of two parts: First a written part. And if you pass that, an oral part. And if you pass that, then you are given the certification.
Question: You are not board certified in any field at all.
Answer: Correct.

. . .

Question: A number of articles that have been published in the literature that you referred to are peer review articles. . . .
Answer: Yes.
Question: . . . in the peer review . . . the editorial board selects those folks who they believe to be sufficiently trained in the area to review articles and offer opinions before [they're] published.
Answer: Correct.
Question: You . . . have not been asked to peer review any article in this area, have you?
Answer: That's correct.

---

to show that the expert's colleagues felt his or her attempted contributions to the field were unworthy of publication.

As important as what is on the curriculum vitae is what is *not* on it. The attorney should consult with other experts in the field to ascertain what credentials and experiences a qualified expert should have. The attorney can then develop a list of all the things this expert witness *is not*. Are there specific organizations that a responsible professional in this line of work should belong to, but this witness does not? Are there licensures missing? Are there experiences that are lacking? The attorney should look for periods of interruptions in the witness's employment history. It might be that the witness was working, but left a particular situation under unfavorable circumstances. That should be explored. It is also possible that the witness might have been unable to work due to professional reasons, such as a suspension in licensing.

Although a witness does not have to be a published author to establish expertise, it may be enlightening for the attorney to see what this expert *has* published. For example, when the expert has published several articles, how many of them pertain to the precise subject matter that is at the heart of this proposed testimony? Many times the irresponsible expert is, indeed, an expert—just not in the particular field in which he or she is now opining.

It may be of significance if the witness has never sought to be published in the area in which he or she claims expertise. It is one thing to offer opinions in court to laypersons; it is another to be willing to have those opinions reviewed by professional colleagues. As one court has noted about expert witnesses: "We know from our judicial experience that many such able persons present studies and express opinions that they might not be willing to express in an article submitted to a refereed journal of their discipline or in other contexts subject to peer review" (*In Re Air Crash Disaster at New Orleans, LA,* 1986, p. 1234).

Additional areas the attorney can check for potentially significant information include continuing professional education credits and professional ethics complaints filed. Generally these are matters of public record.

Continuing education credits demonstrate what advanced study the expert witness has elected to pursue. The records may also reflect upon the expert witness's honesty. This was demonstrated in one case in the cross-examination of an expert witness:

Question: For instance, you told us that you told the State of Oregon that for the year 1987 you attended a program and I think you even made a presentation called *The Use of Polygraph Monitoring* *in the Supervision of Sex Offenders,* and I show you the form you filled out. [Handing papers to the witness]

Answer: Correct.

Question: Now, the very, very first thing you told us in cross-examination was the whole issue of . . . the Court's ability to rely upon what you say is the honesty of your reporting. And that's really what I'm talking about here. You say you went to that seminar and you took credit for eight hours of training. I have a videotape of that seminar. It is three hours long.

Answer: Uh-huh.

Question: You reported eight hours. Why is that, sir?

Applications for state licensing may provide valuable information. One hallmark of the irresponsible expert witness is the attempt to establish credentials beyond his or her true experience. The expert witness sometimes engages in a bit of revisionist history. When this occurs, the information contained in the licensing files can prove helpful, as in this example:

Question: Would this be an accurate description of the work you did there? Just let me know. "Supervision includes discussion of mental health clinic cases, review of clinical work and written materials, discussion of methods of improvement, consultation concerning development of treatment programs and placements. Frequency and duration of supervisory sessions varied depending upon the clinic's consultation schedule." Is that an accurate description of the work you did there?

Answer: Not really.

Question: That's the description that you gave to the State of Oregon when you applied for licensure.

Answer: Yes.

Any source of information that can shed light on the candor of the witness will be of value. In jurisdictions where experts must file affidavits for court funds for payment, those documents should be examined. This can provide some interesting information. For example, these documents were used to cross-examine an expert witness who claimed that DNA evidence was not reliable:

Question: You submitted an affidavit to the Court in this case seeking to get—in support of the defendant's application to get public funds to pay your fee, is that right?

Answer: Yes.

Question: And in that affidavit, did you say—this affidavit was dated February 9, 1989; is that right? Show you a copy if you wish.

Answer: Yes. I can't remember when I did it.

Question: I'm going to show you a four-page document. Does that appear to be your affidavit?

Answer: Yes.

Question: And dated February 9?

Answer: Yes it is.

Question: And you wrote on paragraph four that, "Some officials, most notably John Van de Kamp, Attorney General of California, have warned against getting mesmerized with DNA's potential and slip into a counterproductive scramble to rush the technology from laboratory to courtroom in record time." You indicated that in your affidavit, is that right?

Answer: That's a quote from a speech John Van de Kamp made. Yes, I quoted that.

Question: And he made that speech in January of 1988?

Answer: That's right.

Question: But in January of 1989, in fact two weeks before you submitted this affidavit, Attorney General John Van de Kamp reversed his position on DNA and indicated it was reliable for use in court. Were you aware of that, sir?

Answer: I'm certainly aware of it now. I'm not sure whether I was aware when I did the affidavit or not. I'm not sure. It might have been February when he reversed his position, also.

Mr. Stern: Your honor, I've had marked as Exhibit 48 a photocopy of the *San Francisco Chronicle* dated Wednesday, January 25th, indicating John Van de Kamp approved the use of genetic code technique. I'd offer that into evidence.

The sources of background information on expert witnesses are limited only by the imagination and ingenuity of the attorney.

IS THE EVALUATION PROCESS PROPERLY DONE?

If the witness truly is an expert in the particular field in which he or she is offering an opinion, the inquiry does not stop. The cross-examining attorney should critically explore whether the expert has performed correctly the evaluation pertinent to the case at hand. Factors to consider include the extent to which the expert has adequately utilized proven processes and procedures, relied upon appropriate studies and research, and made logical conclusions based upon facts and information available. In other words, the witness might be skilled enough to know what he or she is doing, but did he or she in fact do it right in this case?

> *The cross-examining attorney should critically explore whether the expert has performed the evaluation correctly.*

Many law school professors and teachers of trial skills argue that in cross-examination the lawyer should never attack the expert witness in the witness's field of expertise.[1] That is not particularly good advice. Indeed, if the lawyer is lazy and does not become familiar with the expert's field, then he or she should not cross-examine the expert in his or her discipline. However, if the attorney does his or her homework, and studies the literature, he or she, can, and should, take on the expert. When the attorney does not challenge the expert about the expert's conclusions, the issue is conceded to the opposing side. It is appropriate, and often necessary, for the cross-examining attorney to challenge the work of the opposing expert witness.

As discussed previously, the trial attorney must take steps to study the expert's field of practice (see the discussion in Chapter 3). The attorney does not need to know the science as well as the expert does, but he or she should know it well enough to recognize when the expert witness has gone beyond what the science can justify.

The attorney should be prepared to contest the methodology used by the witness. For example, if the witness testifies that his or her opinion is based upon a specific test, the attorney should be prepared to question the witness intelligently about the limitations of that test. If the witness testifies that his or her opinion is based upon conclusions of a certain article, the attorney should be prepared to question the witness intelligently about the distinctions in that article. The witness may claim that his or her opinion is based upon sound professional practice, thus the attorney must know what sound professional practice in that discipline really is. The witness may claim that his or her opinion is grounded in good research; the attorney must know whether research findings and methodology truly support the witness's conclusions. For the attorney, an ability to review research articles critically is very helpful (see Williams, Kendall-Tackett, & Stern, 1992).

A word of caution before continuing: Once the attorney learns the material, he or she must carefully consider how best to use it. Once again, the trial attorney should recall the maxim: Just because you can, doesn't mean you should.

The cross-examining attorney

- should know the leading literature in the field and have a working understanding of the material,
- should not ask questions just to demonstrate how smart he or she is,
- should be able to discuss the literature in an intelligent conversation with the expert,
- should never forget that the jury is the audience (the discussion with the expert witness must be understandable to the jurors),
- should have a precise idea of what point or points he or she wants to make in cross-examining the expert, and
- should not ask questions of the expert without having an exact plan of attack.

How to Use the Literature

The attorney must consider in advance what specific articles he or she wants to use in cross-examination. The Federal Rules of Evidence (803 [18]) permit the attorney to ask the expert witness questions about "learned treatises." Cross-examination allows the attorney to bring authoritative material into the courtroom. If the attorney employs such material effectively, he or she can teach the jury as well as impeach the witness. The cross-examining attorney can seek to establish through the use of authoritative writings that the opinions of the expert are at odds with those of persons who are recognized as authorities in the field. At the same time, the attorney can educate the jury about the state of the research or sound professional practice.

In the following example, a psychologist testified in a hearing during a criminal trial that the defendant likely did not commit the alleged child sexual assault, based, in part, on his scores on the Minnesota Multiphasic Personality Inventory (MMPI).[2] The doctor testified that he used the test "to find out the profile characteristics of the pedophile or child abuser or child sexual abuser and compare [the] . . . profile of nonabusers . . . to those that have been found guilty." The doctor then added that the MMPI profile of the defendant showed "he does not fall in the typical profiles of the child sexual abuser or pedophile." The import of this testimony was its implication that the defendant was innocent of the charges based upon his MMPI profile. The cross-examination was designed to show that the respected literature in the field suggests that what this expert did was without support in the research:

Question: Are you familiar with the *Journal of Consulting and Clinical Psychology?*
Answer: Very clearly, that publication, yes.
Question: Is it a revered journal?
Answer: It's a substantial journal.
Question: Are you familiar with an article written by William Erickson, Michael Luxenberg, Nancy Walbek, and Richard Seely dealing with "Frequency of MMPI 2-point Code Types Among Sex Offenders" published in 1987?
Answer: I've seen it, yes.
. . .
Question: That was a study done of 568 individuals who had been convicted of sex offenses; is that correct?
Answer: Um-hmm.
Question: If I understand what you've told us, you can do an MMPI on an individual and tell whether he is an offender. There will be certain characteristics you would expect within the profile; is that correct?
Answer: Yes, probabilities.
Question: Probabilities?
Answer: Um-hmm.

Question: In this study of 568 individuals, more than 19 percent of those who had been convicted of sex offenses had profiles that were perfectly within all normal bounds; is that correct, sir?

Answer: Yes.

Question: This report concludes, does it not, that: " . . . the findings reported here do not support descriptions of any MMPI profile as typical of any sort of sex offender." Is that correct, sir? Is that what the article—

Answer: Yes.

. . .

Question: Are you familiar that this article concludes: "Attempts to identify individuals as likely sex offenders on the basis of the MMPI profiles are reprehensible . . ."

Answer: I wouldn't say reprehensible. I would agree more with their summary abstract. The high—

Question: My question, sir, would you agree that's what this article says?

Answer: Yeah, the article says that.

Question: It says that the practice of identifying individuals as likely sex offenders on the basis of MMPI profiles [is] reprehensible and " . . . represents a serious misuse of the MMPI and it is not supportable by the results of this or any other study." Is that correct, sir?

If a witness recognizes a particular individual to be a leading authority in his or her discipline, the cross-examining attorney should consider contacting that authority before trial. That individual may disagree with the opinions of the witness who is identifying him or her as an authority. In that event, the lawyer might seek to obtain an affidavit, or perhaps even a letter, from that professional, setting forth his or her opinion. That document, although unpublished, may prove to be a useful tool in cross-examining the expert.

IS THE WITNESS AN EXPERT OR AN ADVOCATE?

In addition to evaluating the qualifications of the expert witness and determining whether he or she performed an evaluation in a professionally competent fashion, the cross-examining attorney must also consider whether the opinions of the expert witness should

Using Letters From Others
During Cross-Examination

A medical doctor was testifying on behalf of a criminal defendant in a sexual abuse case in which there was medical testimony of injuries consistent with sexual abuse. The prosecution had reason to believe the defense witness might claim expertise in this field, in part from experience examining children suspected of being victims of sexual abuse referred to him by a local hospital. The prosecutor believed the witness's referrals from that hospital were only of severely injured children. That preparation led to this eventual exchange:

Question: Now you consult at Children's Hospital, right?
Answer: That's right. . . .
Question: What you consult on is issues dealing with surgery; is that right?
Answer: No.
Question: You deal with regular children?
Answer: Yes.
Question: [C.B.] is the person who [makes the referrals to you]?
[The witness in essence agreed.]
. . .
Question: Doctor, I want to give you a letter that was sent to me by Dr. [C.B.] . . . it's been marked as Exhibit 10. I want you to take some time and read it. [Witness complied.]
Question: Would you agree . . . doctor, what your role as a consultant [for] Children's Hospital is, is to see patients with injury which might require surgery?
Answer: That's today.
. . .
Question: . . . the non-acute, the non-serious[ly injured] . . . children who come in with complaints of sexual abuse are not ordinarily referred to you from any hospital in the Pacific Northwest.
Answer: Not under usual circumstances. . . .
Question: And you examine children on a non-acute basis how often?
Answer: Once a year.

The letter that was produced was not introduced into evidence, but was most helpful in keeping the witness honest.

be trusted. Is the expert an unbiased scientist offering sound, objective professional opinions, or an advocate in expert's clothing? Although skepticism might fuel that inquiry, only research and an honest appraisal by the trial lawyer can answer it.

An attorney should not attack anyone's professionalism or honesty without solid evidence. The attorney should endeavor to learn as much as possible about the professional track record of the opposing expert witness. Only when there exists a provable showing of bias on the part of the witness should the attorney make an attack on the witness's objectivity. When such a track record does exist, however, it is the obligation of the trial attorney to expose it.

Decisions made in court are too important to be influenced by those who provide court testimony for personal gain, whether for profit or to advance their own political or social views. Debates regarding social policy should be conducted in academic, legislative, or similar arenas, not in courtrooms, where decisions are made that have serious consequences for individuals and community safety.

This distinction was drawn by one Washington State trial judge. In refusing to allow a well-known expert witness to testify in a particular case, Superior Court Judge John F. Wilson concluded:

> What he's done is evaluate other opinions. He's an advocate for one side more than he is a medical doctor. . . . He's not a clinical or an academic expert; he's a litigation expert. . . . I think more likely he should either be in the legislature to protect people or become a lawyer, which I think he secretly has become, in a sense. (*State v. Werlein*, November 8, 1989)

When the expert witness uses the courtroom to advance a professional or personal agenda, this demonstrates a bias that must be disclosed to the fact finder. No matter how well credentialed an expert might be on paper, extreme bias should render his or her testimony meaningless. As a California judge observed in rejecting the conclusions of an expert witness:

> This court finds that Dr. [Z.] is a very biased witness. His testimony reflects that he has built a cottage industry testifying as an "expert" in cases of this nature. . . . his generalized conclusions are highly disquieting as elitist and unduly self-indulgent and omnipoten[t]. . . .

> Dr. [Z.] brings nothing additional except his extreme bias. . . . Whatever "expertise" he holds as a result of his professional training, such fails to overcome his demonstrated bias, prejudice and inaccurate foundational basis for the opinions expressed during the hearing. (*In Re the Petition of Donna Sue Hubbard*, January 18, 1994)[3]

DISCOVERING THE BIAS

In evaluating whether a witness is truly an expert or an advocate, the attorney should consider the witness's motives for testifying. Some experts seek to advance their own personal or professional agendas; money is often also a prime motivator. Consider this comment by a trial judge in San Luis Obispo, California, who was required to compare the vastly differing testimony by state and defense witnesses in a murder case. Commenting on the defense experts, Judge William Fredman observed: "Each were candid in that a substantial portion of their respective incomes came from testifying against DNA analysis against other scientists all over the nation. This special interest, while not disqualifying of their testimony, cast a pall over it and its objectivity" (*People v. Garcia*, March 25, 1991).

The issue of money was raised again in regard to one of these same witnesses in another case, with that judge remarking: "His financial interest *and* the shifty nature of his criticism gave me considerable pause and I've come to conclude that he seems to fit with that group . . . [that is] . . . a welfare system for academics. Given [the expert's] financial stake, it appears that he's slipped into that" (*People v. Howard*, April 23, 1990).

Clearly, there are some expert witnesses who come into court and express opinions that appear to be motivated by financial rewards for themselves rather than by any earnest desire to provide enlightened contributions of their knowledge. Those people should be exposed as such to the jury.

In the interests of fairness, there is one caution about pursuing this avenue of cross-examination: There is nothing improper about an expert being paid a fee for his or her time. The fact that a particular witness earns a substantial sum of money by testifying or consulting should not, of itself, be considered to be indicative of an irresponsible expert witness. The real issue is whether the expert is an advocate for a particular viewpoint such that his or her opinions are influenced or controlled by the money received from testifying. The attorney needs to explore that possibility.

One avenue for the attorney to explore is whether the witness has contributed to the field of practice other than providing court testimony. Has the witness, for example, conducted independent research, published in peer review journals, written books? Or has the witness conducted no research, and chosen to publish only in those trade journals that are more likely to attract a readership of lawyers than reaction from his or her colleagues?

The lawyer should also take a careful look at the witness's prior court testimony. Does the witness repeat the same points and arguments each time he or she testifies? If those points have been refuted, has the witness done anything to consider the criticisms? The irresponsible expert witness merely continues to say the same things, endures the same cross-examination, then submits a bill for services rendered and moves on to the next courtroom.

Responsible experts pursue better understanding through enhanced academic discussion. Responsible scientists and researchers seek to settle scientific controversies by writing papers, developing better research, and collecting more data. What has this witness done to further the study of the issues in his or her field? Whereas many responsible professionals seek to resolve scientific controversies through more and better research, others profit by the issues' remaining murky enough to maintain the market for their testimony. Some experts do not seek to publish because further discussion of the issues is adverse to their financial stake: If the position the expert witness takes in court testimony is debated in academic settings, a consensus may build, and this could eliminate the market for the witness's testimony. The cross-examining attorney should explore whether the expert witness profits by the prolongation of academic debate in his or her field.

Follow the Money

The cross-examining attorney should endeavor to discover what percentage of income the witness earns from court testimony and legal consultation in comparison with his or her full-time job. The attorney can take steps to determine exactly how much money the particular witness has earned in expert fees. If the attorney cannot easily obtain that figure, he or she must attempt to determine it secondhand. The attorney can ask the witness to disclose all of his or her prior court testimonies, and then can contact the opposing sides in those cases and attempt to ascertain the fees the expert charged. In criminal cases in which the expert witness has been retained by use of public funds, there are likely paper trails in the county's financial records that are matters of public record. These can obviously be valuable sources of information.

Alternatively, during the expert's trial testimony, the attorney can go through each case the expert has been involved in and ask, "How much did you charge for *that* case?" This methodical approach, if effectively done, can be extremely painful for the witness. If ineffectively done, however, it can be extremely boring to the jury.

Follow the Writings

In cases where the expert witness has published, the cross-examining lawyer should attempt to determine whether the expert witness's views have been rebuked by his or her professional colleagues. If the expert has published articles in respected journals, they may have evoked responses. The articles, together with any critical analyses, will help determine whether the views represent a minority or unsubstantiated position. Alternatively, the witness may have been unable to publish in peer review journals because his or her research methodology or reasoning has been poor.

It is important to identify what reactions the experts' peers have had to his or her writings. These might indicate that the "expert" is appearing in court in an attempt to convince laypersons of something he or she has failed to convince his or her professional colleagues of—all for a fee, of course.

❏ An Expert Witness Memorandum

Sometimes the background information obtained on a particular expert witness shows a history of unfavorable comments by trial judges, such as the observations noted above. These opinions by trial judges may be damning remarks, but they are not necessarily of use during cross-examination. There is, however, another way to utilize this material.

In a case in which the trial judge will make a ruling on the admissibility of particular expert testimony, the opposing attorney might consider preparing an *expert witness memorandum*. This document outlines the background of the proposed expert and can provide a forum for detailing the opinions of other trial judges.

The document might summarize the evolution of the expert from academic to expert. It should highlight the professional work the witness has done (or lack thereof). It should emphasize the witness's bias and provide evidence of reasons for that bias. Then, most significantly, it should include comments other judges have made in ruling on the witness's testimony.

For example, in a murder case relying upon DNA evidence, a frequent defense DNA expert was endorsed as a witness for the defendant. The prosecutor filed an expert witness memorandum that indicated its purpose was "to acquaint this court with Dr. [X]." The memorandum detailed some of the proposed witness's background, noting, for example: "None of the articles Dr. [X] has authored which have been published have been subjected to peer review. On the other hand at least two articles he has written which were sent for peer review were thereafter rejected for publication."[4]

The witness's financial stake in the controversy was also discussed: "According to his trial testimonies . . . he has since doubled his hourly fee and has nearly tripled his annual income by being an expert witness against" a particular principle. But the main point of the document was to detail what other judges have said about the particular witness: "Dr. [X] has testified, by his count, in more than 50 cases. Judges across the country have heard his testimony and have been able to compare it with the testimony and knowledge of other experts. Some of those judges have been rather candid in their appraisal of Dr. [X]." Those unfavorable comments were then detailed.

When such an expert witness memorandum has been filed, the trial judge is faced with the opinions of his or her colleagues in considering the proper ruling to make in the instant case.

❏ Practice Considerations

It is virtually impossible to do a professional job cross-examining an expert witness without substantial preparation. Building a thorough cross-examination file takes considerable time. The effort often can, and should, begin long before the witness is endorsed in a particular case.

In most jurisdictions there are certain professionals who often testify for one particular side. Each discipline, it seems, has its select few who practice in what I have referred to above as the Courtroom of Dreams. Local attorneys know who these people are.

Maintaining a file or notebook on all local experts will give the attorney a significant advantage when a specific witness is called as an expert. The attorney should consider collecting as much information as possible on these potential expert witnesses. In particular, the following materials might prove to be helpful:

- Curriculum vitae
- Reports the expert has written
- Articles written by the expert and responses by other professionals
- Trial, hearing, and deposition transcripts
- Court decisions commenting about the expert
- Correspondence with or about the expert
- Bills the expert submitted in prior court cases

In addition to these items, the file should include any and all other information that might reflect on what this individual thinks about and how he or she performs his or her professional work. This material can be gathered and periodically organized for eventual use by the attorney.

The information gathered for such expert witness files is likely to be protected from discovery as attorney work product. See *Dawson v. Daly* (1993), which exempts from public disclosure materials gathered in anticipation of cross-examining an expert witness in "completed, existing or reasonably anticipated litigation" (p. 791).

The gathering of background on potential expert witnesses is significantly easier when attorneys and experts share information. If a particular individual commonly appears as a witness in a general area, professionals in one county might actively exchange information on that person with the attorneys in neighboring counties.

Information on those who are recurrent expert witnesses is also gathered and available from outside sources. For example, the National Center for Prosecution of Child Abuse keeps data and files on many expert witnesses who testify in child abuse cases. Other professional organizations may also maintain reference libraries on specific experts who are proponents of certain viewpoints (for a list of some of these professional associations, see Chapter 2). In specific disciplines, some groups are particularly organized to collect and distribute such information. For example, the American Prosecutory Research Institute also has a DNA Unit that works in junction with the Federal Bureau of Investigation to provide a variety of information on experts who have testified in DNA cases. The attorney needing to confront an opposing expert witness should search out others who have faced that witness before and are willing to share information and strategies.

The attorney can also seek background material by court order. In jurisdictions where it is permissible, the opposing parties should consider discovery demands seeking to uncover specific information. Such requests might be for the following:

- Current and past curricula vitae
- Copies of all the witness's published articles, book chapters, or other writings
- A list of articles that were submitted and rejected for publication (possibly also including peer reviewer comments)
- A list of all cases in which the witness has previously testified
- A list of all journals for which the expert witness has served as a peer reviewer of articles
- A list of all presentations given by the expert in regard to the subject of his or her testimony, including dates, topics, sponsoring organizations, and locations (should include copies of handouts or other written material prepared or disseminated by or on behalf of the witness)

The request should not be overly burdensome or invasive. The point is to obtain information that is truly needed, not to harass a particular witness. In addition, the court is more likely to grant a demand that is reasonable in scope and not an apparent fishing expedition or a request meant to intimidate or annoy the witness.

The attorney should also recognize that if one side files this type of discovery motion, the opposite side might well file a similar motion seeking the same type of information on witnesses. The advice for attorneys is straightforward: Don't ask for anything from the other side that you are not willing to provide for your own witnesses.

❏ A Final Word About Professionalism: The Attack Should Never Get Personal

Although it is appropriate for an attorney to be aggressive in seeking background information about an expert witness, the inquiry should be limited to the witness's professional life. Absent extraordinary circumstances, probing into a witness's personal life is beyond the bounds of fair play.

Likewise, cross-examination should be limited to *professional* issues. No matter how much animosity develops between witness and attorney, the courtroom is a place for *professional* battles. All witnesses in litigation should be afforded respect in the privacy of their personal affairs.

In 1991, a newsletter for private investigators published an article titled "How to Conduct a Thorough Background on Child Abuse Experts, Twenty Easy Steps" (Mailloux, 1991). One of those steps called for delving into "domestic information." Specifically, the article advocated: "Ascertain whether the child abuse expert has been married, has children and who he/she is currently residing with. Although this may seem intrusive, a child abuse expert who does not have children or is gay may have prejudices or biases that are based on assumptions not facts" (p. 5). This kind of investigation is inappropriate in a professional setting. Such an inquiry is overly invasive, is without support in the published research, and has no place in a courtroom.

A thorough cross-examination of the irresponsible expert witness takes considerable preparation and forethought. It takes judgment, self-education, and a firm strategy. It also takes the professionalism to know when certain areas of challenge are inappropriate.

❑ **Notes**

1. See, for example, Wellman (1974): "As a general rule, it is unwise for the cross-examiner to attempt to cope with a specialist in his own field of inquiry" (p. 95).

2. The defendant wanted the witness to testify before the jury. This hearing was an "offer of proof" before the trial judge. After hearing the testimony, the judge substantially limited what the witness could testify to before the jury. The witness was prohibited from testifying about the issue that is the subject of this example. The quotes in text are taken from the testimony of a proposed defense expert witness in *State v. Ross* (1990).

3. The point of this quotation is to illustrate some of the sweeping comments trial courts have made about those perceived as advocates rather than experts. It is not my intent to embarrass this particular witness, and, accordingly, the witness's identity is withheld.

4. As I have noted previously, it is not my intent to embarrass any particular witness. The point of this illustration is to discuss the concept of an expert witness memorandum. Accordingly, the witness's identity is withheld. The memorandum, however, is a matter of public record.

Cases Cited

Commonwealth v. Dunkle, 602 A.2d 830 (Pa. 1992).
Daubert v. Dow, 113 S. Ct. 2786 (1993).
Dawson v. Daly, 845 P.2d 995 (Wash. 1993).
Duckett v. State, 797 S.W.2d 906 (Tex. Ct. App. 1990).
Dutchess County Dept. of Social Services v. Mr. G., 534 N.Y.S.2d. 64 (Fam. Ct. 1988)
Earl M. Kerstetter, Inc., v. Commonwealth, 171 A.2d 163 (Pa., 1961).
Frye v. United States, 54 App.D.C. 46, 293 F. 1013 (1923).
In Re Air Crash Disaster at New Orleans, LA, 795 F.2d 1230 (5th Cir. 1986).
In Re the Petition of Donna Sue Hubbard, Kern County, CA, Case No. 5.5-2738 (1994).
Kelly v. State, 399 S.E.2d 568 (Ga. App. 1990).
Leesona Corp. v. Varta Batteries, Inc., 522 F. Supp. 1304 (S.D.N.Y. 1981).
People v. Beckley, 456 N.W.2d 391 (Mich. 1990).
People v. Garcia, San Luis Obispo, CA, Case No. 15883 (1991).
People v. Howard, Alameda County, CA, Case No. 99217 (1990).
People v. Leahy, 34 Cal.Rptr.2d 663 (Cal. 1994).
People v. Mendible, 245 Cal.Rptr. 553 (1988).
People v. Stoll, 265 Cal.Rptr. 111 (1989).
Rubanick v. Witco Chemical Corp., 576 A.2d 4 (N.J. Super. A.D. 1990).
State v. Batangan, 799 P.2d 48 (Hawaii 1990).
State v. Brown, 802 P.2d 803 (Wash. 1990).
State v. Cauthron, 846 P.2d 502 (1993).
State v. Jackson, 721 P.2d 232 (Kansas 1986).
State v. Lord, 822 P.2d 117 (Wash. 1991), *cert. denied,* 113 S. Ct. 164 (1992).
State v. Maule, 667 P.2d 96 (Wa. Ct. App., 1983).
State v. Milbradt, 756 P.2d 620 (Or. 1988).
State v. Owens, 913 P.2d 366 (Wash. 1996).

State v. Ross, Snohomish County, WA, Cause No. 89-1-01380-5 (1990).

State v. St. Hilaire, 775 P.2d 876 (Or. App. 1989).

State v. Smith, 564 P.2d 1154 (Wash. 1977).

State v. Swan, 790 P.2d 610 (Wash. 1990).

State v. Werlein, Snohomish County, WA, Cause No. 88-1-01148-1 (1989).

Townsend v. State, 734 P.2d 705 (Nev. 1987).

Trower v. Jones, 520 N.E.2d 297 (Ill. 1988).

U.S. v. Crumby, 895 F. Supp. 1354 (D. Ariz., 1995).

U.S. v. Pierre, 812 F.2d 417 (8th Cir. 1987).

Van Blargan v. Williams Hospitality Corp., 754 F. Supp. 246 (D. Puerto Rico, 1991).

References

Adams, J. (1993). Classification of anogenital findings in children with suspected sexual abuse: An evolving process. *APSAC Advisor, 6*(2), 11-13.

Bailey, F. L. (1985). *To be a trial lawyer.* New York: John Wiley.

Buckley, J. A. (1992). The prosecution's use of social science expert testimony in child sexual abuse cases: National trends and recommendations. *Journal of Child Sexual Abuse, 1*(2), 75-95.

Cleary, E. (Ed.). (1972). *McCormick's handbook on the law of evidence.* St. Paul, MN: West.

De Parcq, W. H. (1956). Law, science and the expert witness. *Tennessee Law Review, 24,* 166-171.

Elliott, D. (1987). Science panels in toxic tort litigation: Why we don't use them. In *ICET Symposium III Immunotoxicology: From lab to lab.* Ithaca, NY: Cornell University, Institute for Comparative and Environmental Toxicology.

Ferguson, R., & Fine, S. A. (1990). *Washington practice, criminal law.* St. Paul, MN: West.

Griffin, F. H. (1961). Impartial medical testimony: A trial lawyer in favor. *Temple Law Quarterly, 34,* 402-415.

Heger, A., & Emans, S. J. (1992). *Evaluation of the sexually abused child.* New York: Oxford University Press.

Levy, E. S. (1961). Impartial medical testimony—revisited. *Temple Law Quarterly, 34,* 416-451.

Louisell, D. W., & Mueller, C. B. (1992). *Federal evidence* (Suppl.). San Francisco: Bancroft-Whitney.

Mailloux, B. (1991, December). How to conduct a thorough background on child abuse experts, twenty easy steps. *The Investigator,* pp. 3-5.

Model criminal jury instructions for the Ninth Circuit (Federal Court). (1994). St. Paul, MN: West.

Murphy, W., & Peters, J. (1992). Profiling child sexual abusers: Psychological considerations. *Criminal Justice and Behavior, 19*, 24-37.

Myers, J. E. B. (1992). *Evidence in child abuse and neglect cases* (2nd ed.). New York: John Wiley.

Myers, J. E. B., Bays, J., Becker, J., Berliner, L., Corwin, D., & Saywitz, K. (1989). Expert testimony in child sexual abuse litigation. *Nebraska Law Review, 68*, 1-34.

National Center for Prosecution of Child Abuse. (1993). *Investigation and prosecution of child abuse* (2nd ed.). Alexandria, VA: National District Attorneys Association, American Prosecutors Research Institute.

Specter (1987, July 28). Diagnosis or verdict? Psychiatrists on the witness stand? *Washington Post.*

Stern, P. (1994). Science in the courtroom: From the Frye-pan to the fire. *Violence Update, 4*(12), 5-6.

Summit, R. (1992). Misplaced attention to delayed memory. *APSAC Advisor, 5*(3), 21-25.

Wecht, C. H. (Ed.). (1993). *Forensic sciences* (Vol. 4). New York: Matthew Bender.

Wellman, F. (1974). *The art of cross-examination.* New York: Collier.

Williams, L. M., Kendall-Tackett, K., & Stern, P. (1992). A practitioner's guide to interpreting research results. *APSAC Advisor, 5*(2), 1, 12-14.

Index

American Professional Society on the
   Abuse of Children (APSAC), 40,
   50, 113
Analogies, use of, 75, 83-84

Bibliography of recommended
   readings, 51-52

Case review by the expert,
   obtaining the full file, 60-61, 144-
   148
Code of Judicial Conduct, 10
Confidentiality between patient and
   expert, 127-130
Consulting experts, 42-43, 119
Court appointed experts, 43-44
Cross-examination, *See* generally
   Chapter 5.
   affidavits for court funds, 158,
   163-164
   answering yes or no, 100-101,
   153-154
   applications for state licensure, 163

challenging qualifications of the
   witness, 158-165
membership in organizations, 160
misleading questions, 103-105
professional education credits,
   162-163
professionalism, 177-178
regarding fees, 112-114, 171-173
regarding lifestyle, 102, 177-178
regarding literature, 105-108, 166-168
reviewing curriculum vitae, 159-163
seven rules for experts, 95
use of humor, 110-111
Curriculum vitae,
   defined, 31-32
   double-checking for accuracy by
   witness, 32, 142
   obtaining by attorney, 158-159
   verification by cross-examining
   attorney, 159-163

Daubert v. Dow, 16-17, 22
Degree of certainty of opinion, 92-93
DNA evidence, 55

About the Author

Paul Stern is Senior Deputy Prosecuting Attorney for Snohomish County, Washington. He has been a prosecutor since 1981, and has tried dozens of cases of child sexual abuse, physical abuse, and child homicide, as well as many other murder, assault, and rape cases. He serves on the Executive Committee of the Board of Directors for the American Professional Society on the Abuse of Children and is Past President of the Washington Professional Society on the Abuse of Children. He was appointed to the Governor's Advisory Committee on DNA and currently serves on the Sexual Offender Treatment Provider Advisory Committee. He is a frequent lecturer at conferences dealing with child abuse and neglect issues, and has testified several times before legislative committees on these topics. He has published several articles about expert witnesses and child abuse issues, and has served as legal editor for the *APSAC Advisor* and *Violence Update;* he is currently on the editorial board of *Child Maltreatment.* A graduate of Ithaca College and Rutgers-Camden Law School, he is admitted to practice law in Washington and New Jersey, and before the U.S. Supreme Court.

About the Contributor

Benjamin E. Saunders is Associate Professor in the Department of Psychiatry and Behavioral Sciences at the Medical University of South Carolina in Charleston, where he directs the Family and Child Program of the National Crime Victims Research and Treatment Center. He received his Ph.D. in clinical social work from Florida State University and has a master's degree in marriage and family therapy from Virginia Tech. He is a licensed independent social worker and a licensed marriage and family therapist, and he serves on the editorial boards of *Child Maltreatment, Journal of Child Sexual Abuse, Journal of Family Social Work,* and the *APSAC Advisor.* His research on crime victims, offenders, and incest families has been funded by federal agencies such as the National Institute of Mental Health, the National Institute of Justice, the National Institute on Drug Abuse, and the National Center on Child Abuse and Neglect. In addition to his research and teaching activities, he maintains an active clinical and consulting practice with victims of sexual assault, family members of victims, and sexual offenders, and often is called as an expert witness in legal cases.